WHAT THE MEDIA IS SAYING

"This is a must read for seniors and ~~~ ~~~ult children. Best preventive problem bo~~~ ~~~ written."

— **Sonny Bloch, host of America's long~~~ ~~~ing nationally syndicated financia~~~ ~~~w**

"Harley Gordon's book is bound to save American families untold anguish as well as millions of dollars. It is must reading for anyone with an aging parent."

— **Terry Savage**
***Terry Savage Talks Money*, WBBM -TV (CBS)**
Chicago Sun Times

"The best book on the subject."

— **Ken and Daria Dolan, authors and radio/TV hosts**
***Smart Money*, CNBC; *Talknet;* WOR-AM, NY**

"This compassionate attorney explains how, by understanding the law, people can save a significant amount of their assets, including their homes."

— *Golden Years Magazine*

"A superb job of creating order out of chaos."

— *Mass. Lawyers Weekly*

"Easy to read ... explains clearly some of Medicaid's most complex inscrutabilities."

– *Library Journal*

"Simply written and well-designed ... to help make Medicaid planning options approachable by the nonprofessional reader."

– *United Retirement Bulletin*

"Stripped of the frills, the message [is] pretty simple: If you plan, you and your family can hold on to your money; if you don't it could all go to pay for a nursing home."

– *The Boston Globe*

"*How to Protect Your Life Savings* gives us in simple and accessible terms, most of the information we need about a subject we would rather not deal with – but almost surely will have to."

– *Doris Dawson*
former Chair of the Board of National Gray Panthers

How to PROTECT Your Life Savings From Catastrophic Illness and Nursing Homes

How to
PROTECT
Your Life
Savings

From Catastrophic Illness and Nursing Homes

HARLEY GORDON
Attorney at Law
with
Jane Daniel

FINANCIAL PLANNING INSTITUTE, INC.
BOSTON, MA

Second Edition
First Edition Published 1990

Designed by Daniel & Daniel
        Ronald Duce
        Suzanne Lucien
        Dennis Fonte
Cover: Battles Design

Printed in the United States of America
ISBN 0-9625667-1-3

FINANCIAL
PLANNING
INSTITUTE

FINANCIAL PLANNING INSTITUTE, INC.
P.O. Box 135
Boston, MA 02258
(617) 965-8120

Acknowledgments

The practice of elder law didn't exist ten years ago. It was through the efforts of a group of talented, committed attorneys that this service, including Medicaid planning, exists today. They include:

Cynthia Barrett, Robert Freedman, Natalie J. Kaplan, DeCosta Mason, Harriet Prensky, Patricia A. Smith, Barbara M. Wertheimer, Alan Bogutz, Nancy Solnick, Scott Severns, M. Gary Eakes.

Special thanks and affection go to attorneys Alexander Bove, Michael Gilfix, Tim Nay, Vincent J. Russo (and Theresa), Mark Woolpert, and Peter Strauss, friend and mentor.

The charts in the back of the book were compiled through the assistance of both private attorneys and state Medicaid offices. Thank you all for your help.

Special acknowledgment is given to Brian Barreira and Ann Weber who generously shared their knowledge of the tax system.

Gratitude to Sheila Sennett Allen for sharing her knowledge. The section entitled "A Man Away from Poverty" is based on material she provided.

AUTHOR'S NOTE

What will this book give you?

Knowledge.
Knowledge equals power.
And power equals CONTROL.

We all struggle to keep control over our lives and our assets. Knowledge is the key to control. We learn how to invest, how to save and when to change course. We struggle to maintain our balance.

If you are facing a catastrophic illness, you are beginning to realize what a loss of control can do to your life. Loss of control over your assets is usually not far behind. Lack of knowledge about how to protect life savings exposes you to financial ruin.

Most self-help books encourage you to do-it-yourself. In this area, it's not a good idea. My assumption is that you *will* need professional help. After reading this book, you will have identified the difficult points which an attorney can help resolve. The wide margins are for you to make notes. Mark this book and take it with you when you see a lawyer.

It is not the intention of this book to encourage you to hide all your assets and claim poverty. You have a responsibility to pay your fair share. It is my intent to help you protect the balance of your assets and, in particular, your house.

In lecturing to audiences of professional and senior citizens' groups, I have seen that they have one thing in common — everyone's confused. This manual is written to clear up the confusion. It tells you in simple language not just what the problem is but what you can do about it. It explains the laws, but there isn't a word of "legalese" on these pages.

You may notice that there is some repetition of certain points. That's intentional. Many people go right to the chapter that pertains to their situation, without reading all the background information. We give it to them again so they won't miss anything.

The solutions offered here are not textbook answers. Instead, I have drawn upon my experiences and those of other professionals whom I trust to give you a street-wise understanding of a complex and sometimes bizarre system.

In the months since this book first came out, readers and audiences have raised other points they'd like to know more about. This expanded edition includes responses to those questions.

After reading this book, you can make your decisions, however painful and difficult they may be, with confidence that you are acting in an informed and responsible manner.

Harley Gordon

TABLE OF CONTENTS

4   **HOW TO PROTECT ASSETS WHEN THERE IS TIME TO PLAN**   **63**

5

WHAT TO DO WHEN YOU DON'T HAVE TIME TO PROTECT YOUR ASSETS 113

6

PROTECTING INCOME FROM MEDICAID 139

TABLE OF CONTENTS

TABLE OF CONTENTS

TABLE OF CONTENTS

17 RESOURCES 261

LAWYER REFERRAL FORM 275

Whose problem is this?

We are hearing a lot about nursing homes and their cost these days. We hear that nursing homes are expensive. We hear that old people are going into nursing homes and the the taxpayers have to pick up the cost. With the current squeeze on state and federal budgets, people are getting upset at what appears to be yet another drain on the taxpayers' dollars.

What's really happening?

The answer is that we are facing a period of tremendous social change. As we near the end of the century, a national crisis is being played out in the homes of average families all across America. You are contributing to the crisis if you watch your cholesterol, exercise, take your vitamins, and see your doctor regularly, because you are probably going to live longer. In fact, more and more people are living longer. In the next 40 years, the population of people over 65 will almost double. Today, the fastest growing segment of the population is people 85 and older.

That's what's causing the crisis. With increasing age come more frailty and illness. On an individual level, families all over the country are coming face to face with sweeping social change as they struggle to take care of the aging members of their families.

When their elders fall victim to a catastrophic illness like a stroke or Alzheimer's disease, families try to take care of them as best and as long as they can. To do it, family members often give up their normal way of life and their peace of mind. Marriages are stressed to the breaking point; children live with constant tension. Taking care of a chronically ill person at home makes the whole family chronically ill.

The idea that selfish people are dumping their relatives in nursing homes is pure myth. In fact, 85 percent of the frail elderly are cared for at home. Of the remaining 15 percent, half have no immediate family and the rest usually have relatives who are themselves frail and elderly.

The problem of coping with a serious illness can be so painful the people who haven't experienced it can hardly imagine it. Every year, a million families struggle against heartbreak and exhaustion and finally give up. In the end, they make what many call the most painful decision of their lives: they put a beloved spouse or parent in a nursing home.

But the tragedy doesn't end there. Medicare and private insurance do not cover the cost of long-term care. When one spouse is admitted to a nursing home, in only a few weeks or months, on average, the couple's entire life savings are wiped out.

Then, when their savings are gone, Medicaid, a program for poor people who have no other means to pay, steps in to pick up on the nursing home cost. The state determines how much money the well spouse is allowed to keep. For people of modest means, the well spouse will be impoverished and may live out the remainder of his or her life perilously close to, or below, the poverty line.

For both spouses, the sick and the well, control over their money is gone, and with it goes the dignity, security and independence they worked all their lives to attain. It's terrifying. As one elderly woman put it, "I wake up every morning in fear."

This does not have to happen. In fact, social policy recognizes that impoverishment is a bad thing. Therefore, the law allows us to avoid financial ruin. There are a number of strategies to do this, like putting assets in trust or giving them away, but until recently, few people knew about them.

When assets are protected this way, there is no safety net, in the form of private insurance or public entitlement programs, to bridge the gap. Should a catastrophic illness strike, Medicaid, a form of welfare, is all that's left to pick up the cost.

And that makes many taxpayers furious. Their argument goes, "I don't want my tax dollars to pay for your mother's nursing home bill." In short, "It's your problem; you handle it."

Given the seriousness of the threat, people need to have a way to protect themselves. Unfortunately, there's almost nothing that responsible people can do, other than to use whatever legal means are available to protect their assets.

Private insurance is not the answer for people of modest means because nursing home policies are too expensive.

A disturbing number of these policies are riddled with restrictions, exceptions, and deliberate fuzzy language that disqualifies the policy-holder from ever collecting much of anything.

Another insurance trap is that most policies provide insufficient or no defense against the erosion of benefits by the rising cost of health care. If you buy a nursing home policy today and are institutionalized in ten years, it is unlikely that you will have enough benefits to cover more than a small fraction of your nursing home bill.

Many states have adopted regulations to try to eliminate the worst abuses, but senior citizens' groups feel that the effort hasn't gone nearly far enough.

In addition to these drawbacks, the policies are too expensive for the vast majority of seniors. Of all older Americans between the ages of 65 and 79, a whopping 84 percent cannot afford to pay the average cost of basic nursing home insurance policies from nine leading companies, according to one recent study.

So what some people are doing is protecting themselves as best they can by using the provisions available under the law. Are these people "flimflamming Medicaid" by taking advantage of loopholes to dump their relatives onto the taxpayers backs? Are they welfare free-loaders, "false poor" riding a "gravy train," as one national magazine asserts?

Here's a typical story:

My father died from a hereditary disorder that caused a long, slow degeneration of his mind and body. I helped my mother care for him till he mercifully suffered a fatal stroke. I'm convinced that the enormous effort contributed to my mother's death a year after his.

Now I am at risk for the disease. I am 16 years older than my wife. I have two children and a disabled brother who depends upon us for assistance, financial and otherwise.

My wife inherited a house from her mother. We both work full-time and try to save money for our old age. With two children and my brother, it isn't easy to put money aside. I worry constantly about how my family will manage if I develop the disease. I have to do everything I can, now, to protect them if something happens to me.

This case is the norm, not the exception. Sure, there are probably a few wealthy people with high-priced lawyers and accountants who are getting their relatives on Medicaid. True, Medicaid was designed to provide for the poor who have no other means to pay for long-term care. But that's the point — there is no system there for the middle class. Does that mean that it makes sense to drive millions of elderly Americans into poverty before we lend them a hand?

Most people accept responsibility for dealing with misfortunes that befall them, even those which occur through no fault of their own. Most people are willing to pay their fair share.

But what is a fair share? What does society owe to the millions of hard-working senior citizens whose taxes have carried this country's economy for half a century? There is no blame or culpability here. Catastrophic illness is an act of God. People do not choose to become critically ill.

When they have outlived their good health and independence, should society say, "Hey, it's your problem; you handle it?"

This issue is a one of the biggest challenges we face as we move toward the next century. It is an individual problem; it is a social problem: Where does responsibility lie? We are being called upon to examine our fundamental beliefs about ourselves and our society.

We operate on the basic assumption that it is the individual's responsibility to society to work for the greatest good for the greatest number. That's why we obey the laws and pay our taxes.

Conversely, it is society's responsibility to the individual to do the same. The whole, in its magnitude, promotes the well-being of the individual. That's why, when an earthquake, hurricane or other act of God strikes, our collective taxes and insurance reserves pay for disaster relief. But when catastrophic illness strikes, there is no adequate "disaster relief."

Senior citizens have held up their end of the bargain. We as a society are not holding up ours.

The problem, in the proportions we are witnessing today, is new. Government and private industry have not yet come up with the answers. Until they do, individuals must use whatever legal means are available to protect themselves.

A man away from poverty

Mary Ellen, a former secretary, was widowed at age 65. Her husband's pension provided survivor benefits. With that income and her social security, she was able to manage. Four years later she married Joe, a retired factory worker, who had his own pension. Her former husband's pension benefits terminated when she remarried.

A year later, Joe suffered a stroke. As months went by, medical bills piled up. When Joe died three years later, Mary Ellen faced staggering medical bills. Worse, she learned to her dismay that Joe's pension did not cover her because she had not been married to Joe at the time he was employed. After a lifetime of hard work, Mary Ellen now lives below the poverty line.

The economic problems facing senior citizens today are even worse for women than for men. Women make up a shocking 82 percent of poor elders living alone.

There are a number of complex and changing social, economic and demographic factors behind this statistic. For one, women tend to marry men who are older; therefore the husband's health may begin to fail before the wife's. To compound the problem, her life expectancy is 7 years longer than his. She may be on her own, perhaps in failing health herself, for more than a decade after her husband is out of the picture.

Another factor: Because traditionally the male's role is to manage the family finances, a woman is often poorly equipped to cope with financial matters when her husband becomes ill or dies. In fact, many men are even secretive about their financial affairs.

In second marriages, the old model of "older man, younger woman" may be even more exaggerated, with the wife being a decade or two younger than her husband. In any case, for people of modest means, assets are decimated if he goes into a nursing home.

Our social systems, designed for a simpler time, were geared to a population in which most women spent their lives in the home. In addition, people lived relatively short lives by today's standard (rarely past 60). It was assumed that women's economic well-being for their whole adult lives would be provided by their husbands. Unfortunately, today that assumption often proves to be untrue.

The death of a husband often devastates the wife financially as well as emotionally because women have fewer resources to secure their old age. They rely heavily on their spouse's pension and health insurance, one or both of which may terminate when he dies. Many husbands don't choose survivor benefits on their pension plans. At the very least, when the husband dies, benefits are greatly reduced.

Historically, those women who worked outside the home were not as well compensated as men. A woman made only 64 cents for every dollar a man earned in 1939. Pensions and fringe benefits were practically non-existent.

Today, less than one in four women receive pensions at all, and even at that they get only about two-thirds of what men receive. The average woman's pension barely covers utility bills in today's economy.

By the way, women who are currently employed outside the home will face the same problems when they retire. For all the lip service paid to women's equality, for all the good intentions, women's earnings as compared to men's have risen by only 2 cents!

But what about social security? Doesn't that help

older women?

Not necessarily. This public program serves women as ineffectively as private pensions. Due to lower earnings and shorter periods of employment, women's individual social security income is less than men's. And the system is fundamentally unfair to working women. Ironically, women who worked and paid into social security for years may actually receive less than some married women who receive half of their husband's allowance although they never held a job.

On the other side, a married woman whose husband's health gives out has her own set of problems. Matters get completely out of hand with the onset of a long-term illness. At first, the couple's savings are used on special nurses and equipment and remodeling to keep the spouse at home. A couple who may have been able to live comfortably on income generated by savings and pensions will now find their funds strained to provide for his illness.

That's the beginning of the end. Older people rely on the income generated by their savings to live on. With finances already crumbling under medical burdens, the husband goes into the nursing home. Medicaid then requires the couple to "spend down" a major portion of whatever savings they have left. The wife now finds herself with too little monthly income to make ends meet. Because she is getting older herself and is emotionally stressed, her own medical expenses may be rising. Bit by bit, as she dips into the principal, she further reduces her income, till finally she has to sell her house.

When assets such as a home or a bank account are used to cover the cost of a husband's final illness, the woman is left to face the last years of her own life alone, with scant income, nothing in reserve and sometimes no place to live.

A study conducted by the National Bureau of Economic Research found that half of poor widows were not poor before their husbands died. Loss of income from pensions and the burden of medical and funeral costs pushed them over the edge.

Our social policies have failed to keep pace with economic and demographic changes, leaving older women facing terrible financial risks, "a man away from poverty."

Many men of the 65-plus generation pride

themselves on their lifelong ability to provide for their wives and families. It is a cruel irony that many of them will leave behind a widow who may barely survive on her own.

It's legal, but is it right?

Let's get one thing straight: There is nothing, NOTHING, that middle-class seniors detest more than the idea of being on Medicaid. Call it what you will, this system has the shame and stigma of welfare all over it.

For people who've prided themselves on a lifetime of independence and self-sufficiency, taking Medicaid is accepting defeat. The reason they do it is because they usually have to, sooner or later.

A vulnerable existence, the elderly's daily lives are made easier or more difficult by the machinations of huge social systems that protect some of them and allow others to fall through the cracks.

Today, there are a couple of systems that are working quite well for the elderly. One, social security, is an entitlement program that guarantees income after retirement. The word entitlement means that everybody who has held a job and paid social security taxes is entitled to benefits, generally in rough proportion to their contributions. For many, this program alone has provided whatever financial security they have in their old age.

Another system, Medicare, is also an entitlement program that benefits the elderly. Those who have paid into the system receive assistance with medical bills. For all its awkward paperwork and incomplete coverage, older people are grateful for the protection, albeit incomplete, that Medicare provides.

Since the benefits of both these programs are available to the vast majority of elderly, regardless of whether their present financial status is sound or shaky, neither stigmatizes the receivers of the systems' largesse. "Assisting all, they humiliate none," according to Richard Margolis in his book, *Risking Old Age in America*.

Not so Medicaid. Medicaid is a means-tested assistance program, with about 70 percent of its disbursements going to the elderly. "Means tested" means one must *qualify* to receive assistance. In order to qualify, one must be abjectly poor.

This is how Margolis describes Medicaid:

> ...whereas it is mainly Medicare that serves the middle-class elderly in their pursuit of affordable health care, it is chiefly Medicaid that abets their financial struggles in nursing homes. But by that time they are no longer middle-class — they are destitute. For a salient feature of Medicaid is that it does nothing to dispel poverty; it manufactures it...

> Medicaid is a crucible for downward mobility, compelling families to "spend down" their assets before the government will consent to prop them up. "Spend down" is a government euphemism for parting with one's social security and life savings, and in most cases the process is not lengthy.

According to a recent study by the House Select Committee on aging, within one year, over 90 percent of elderly nursing home residents had depleted their assets and incomes and were impoverished. For two-thirds of single people, the loss occurs in a matter of weeks.

For married people, surviving spouses are left to face the remainder of their lives perilously close to the brink of poverty. The Spousal Impoverishment Act of 1989 sought to correct this problem by setting aside a portion of the couple's assets and income for the at-home spouse.

It is still too early to tell if that allowance actually will permit most surviving spouses to elude financial dependency for the remainder of their lives. The figures, however, are not reassuring.

About 40 percent of people over 65 make less than $10,000 a year. This is the class of invisible elderly poor. Over a third more make between $10,000 and $30,000. These people live in daily fear for their financial security. A serious illness or the death of a spouse can tip them suddenly into poverty.

Nor is the next rung on the financial ladder well secured. Even for this relatively affluent group with income between $30,000 and $50,000 a year, a long-term illness can mean catastrophe. With nursing homes costing about that much annually, even for this group impoverishment can occur with stunning speed.

What we see here is that virtually the entire senior population is financially vulnerable. Juxtapose that picture against this one: In the 65-plus age group, almost half will spend time in a nursing home, most for between a year and five years or more.

The collision of these two forces, widespread financial vulnerability and massive long-term care needs, will create destitution for millions at a time in their lives when their capacity to recover is at its lowest ebb. As each victim falls into the maws of the problem, he drags other family members, spouses and dependents, closer to the brink of poverty.

The Spousal Impoverishment Act sought to sever this destructive connection by setting aside enough money to maintain the surviving spouse. Most of those survivors will be women who will face a decade or more alone after their marital assets have been decimated in caring for their husbands. Their financial security will be so precarious that the burden of relatively routine medical expenses will set the whole downward slide in motion again with them as its victims.

It is a short-sighted economy in which the government rushes in to seize assets as soon as one spouse falls, only to leave the survivor so vulnerable that sooner or later, perhaps inevitably, she herself ends up on the public dole.

For taxpayers, it's a question of pay now or pay later, but it is still government that will have to pay. Considering the decade or more of life expectancy in which the widow may need assistance, perhaps if the government took less now, it would have to pay less later.

Middle class people worry about using Medicaid to protect themselves from financial devastation. They may know it's legal, but they feel it isn't "right." Medicaid is, after all, welfare. The stigma associated with welfare adds insult to injury. But for many, the alternative to using Medicaid now is the likelihood of needing it just a little farther down the line.

As a society we must develop a more humane program, guaranteeing to all protection from the financial ravages of long-term illness. By raising the threshold, we can allow people to qualify for assistance with more dignity. In the words of Richard Margolis:

> We must look at ways to take the sting out of Medicaid assistance. When the price of rescue

is pauperization, the rescue itself becomes compromised. The practice of compulsory "spending down" is a throwback to the days of almshouses and public auctions. It makes no sense in a civilized modern society, much less in the world's richest nation.

Excerpts from *Risking Old Age in America* by Richard Margolis, published 1989, are reprinted by permission from Westview Press, Boulder, Colorado.

THE PROBLEM

At the turn of the century, the average life expectancy in the United States was 47 years. As we reach the last decade of this century, life expectancy has increased to 75 years and people commonly live much longer. By the year 2030, the 65-plus population will more than double; one in every five Americans will be 65 or older. The longer we live, the more we become susceptible to frailties and illnesses that may incapacitate rather than kill us. As a society and as individuals we are facing some fundamental questions in our struggle to care for an expanding older population.

One of the major problems is: Who takes care of us when we can't manage on our own anymore? Who takes care of our parents? Who takes care of people who are so incapacitated that they need long-term custodial attention?

More and more, the answer is a nursing home. Nursing homes provide long-term custodial care for conditions or illnesses that incapacitate a person— Alzheimer's and related senile dementia, Parkinson's disease, crippling rheumatoid arthritis, stroke, and other major disabilities.

According to a recent study published in *The New England Journal of Medicine*, of people who turned 65 in 1990, a whopping 43 percent will enter a nursing home at some time before they die. More than half of those people will spend at least a year there, and almost a quarter will spend at least five years of their lives there. Those are sobering statistics.

The costs are just as disturbing. In the Northeast, the cost of a nursing home bed can run up to $60,000 a year. Although the cost may be less in other parts of the country, income and savings are proportionately less as well. Few people can afford those kinds of expenses out-of-pocket.

Ultimately the question arises: Who pays for long-term nursing home care? As we will see, there are few sources available.

The harsh realities

When a serious illness strikes a family member, relatives go into emotional shock. The last thing they think about is the financial aspects of long-term disability. It may seem distasteful, insensitive, or even crass to talk about money with someone who has just been diagnosed as having a long-term debilitating and possibly fatal disease.

Spouses are emotionally devastated by the thought that their life partner will one day be incapacitated and need a nursing home. Family members may have as much difficulty talking with the well spouse as with the person who is ill. Even though some members of the family may realize that a good, honest discussion is in order, it's one thing to know it and quite another to do it.

The problem of talking about finances and making plans is particularly difficult when it is the husband who has been stricken. Most elderly couples have enjoyed traditional marriages in which the wife's role was one of dutiful homemaker and the husband's one of active provider. Though their roles are equally important, one of the consequences of this arrangement is that the wife has generally had little or no experience in managing assets or taking care of finances. The worst time for her to learn about money is when she hears that her spouse has a debilitating illness that will ultimately put him in a nursing home.

This situation, combined with a strong denial instinct in the face of pain, postpones the time when the couple seeks or accepts help in finding ways to protect themselves financially. Inaction can mean that a lifetime of accumulated assets is wiped out because of an illness over which no one has any control.

Heartbreaking stories, painful decisions

Mr. A. was diagnosed as having Parkinson's disease. Mr. and Mrs. A.'s daughter, Gloria, tried to talk with her mother about her dad's worsening condition and what plans they should be making for the time when she and her mother could no longer care for him at home. Gloria tried to find times when her mother seemed open to discussing the topic. But whenever the subject was raised, Mrs. A. became agitated and walked out of the room. Mrs. A. could not face the probability that her husband's illness would one day require nursing home care. The nature of the illness itself supported that denial because of its slow and insidious development. Despite the fact that the symptoms were becoming more pronounced, the mother failed to see what the daughter could see all too clearly. Gloria knew that her father was getting worse and that her mother was withdrawing, unable to make any decisions, unsure of what to do next.

Open communication is difficult under the stress of a serious illness but it is essential to planning for long-term care. And when the relationship between one or both parents and their offspring was never particularly close, the difficulties are compounded. Over the years personality clashes develop and disappointments set in on both sides.

Communication problems usually have nothing to do with the love that the parents and children feel for each other. But because of these difficulties, when the diagnosis of a catastrophic illness is made, the children may not even be informed. The offspring may go along for months sensing something is wrong with their mother or father and not knowing what to do about it. One of the toughest discussions a person can ever have with a parent starts with the question, "What's wrong?"

Robert L. had suspected for a year that his father had Alzheimer's. Robert had never had a warm relationship with his father and ever since his mother's death they had drifted apart. Because of their lack of closeness, Robert was unable to talk with his father about his concern over the old man's health, and his father was unable to ask his son for help. Together they were both victims. Robert felt anguish over his father's worsening condition. His pain was complicated by the worry that, as an only child, he would have to be the one to put his dad in a nursing home and find a way to pay for it.

Another difficult situation sometimes occurs where unmarried siblings are involved. Elderly people who have chosen not to marry tend to be self-reliant. What family ties they have are usually to brothers and sisters. (It's surprising how many of these people never married because they chose instead to take care of an aging parent.) While the siblings may be independent, it is not uncommon for them to hold their assets together. And although they are close, that doesn't mean that they plan together or tell each other everything.

Dolores and Edna were sisters who lived around the corner from each other. One night, at 2:00 am, Edna was awakened by a call from the police. An officer had found Dolores wandering down the middle of the street in her nightgown. As close as they were, her sister never confided to her what Edna had suspected for many months: Dolores was losing her faculties. Edna knew she had to get help for her sister because Dolores was putting herself in danger. But what would it cost and how would the bills be paid? All their money was held jointly, so what affected Dolores also affected Edna.

Sometimes a situation is thrust upon a family member who never expected it. When unmarried or widowed elderly people survive their siblings, who makes the arrangements for care when it's needed? Often it is a favorite niece or nephew, the one they treated as one of their own. Nephews and nieces are usually completely in the dark about the older generation's financial affairs. What they know is generally limited to what they learned at Thanksgiving and Christmas celebrations.

William knew for years that his Aunt Claire suffered from chronic depression. Somehow she always took care of herself so the problem was never addressed. Aunt Claire never acknowledged that there was anything wrong. One day, William received a phone call from her doctor (she'd given his name as next of kin): "Would you be willing to be your aunt's guardian?" he was asked. He wasn't too surprised that she was failing. What bothered him was that he had no idea how to face or help her, and what resources were available to provide for her care in a nursing home if it became necessary.

The previous illustrations show the various and difficult ways that people come face to face with the problem of catastrophic illness. Facing the facts of the situation as quickly as possible is of major importance because *the options are limited and timing is crucial.* The alternative to dealing effectively with the financial implications of a major illness is devastation for the family both monetarily and emotionally.

People work and struggle a lifetime to set aside enough to provide security for themselves and their offspring. The first step in dealing with the problem of protecting assets from chronic illness and long-term nursing home care is to learn about it. Knowledge is the best preparation for confronting the problem head on.

We will look at ways to protect assets in two scenarios:

First: When there is time to plan because the illness has been diagnosed early and progresses slowly.

Second: When there is a crisis, such as a stroke or an accident that requires long-term care immediately.

CHAPTER 2

ALTERNATIVES TO NURSING HOMES

Continuing care retirement communities

In the past several years, there has been a nationwide proliferation of retirement communities. Developers who want to cash in on the burgeoning population of elderly people are agressively marketing this relatively new product. Many of these facilities promise to care for you for the rest of your life, even if your health fails and you become incapacitated. Are life care communities an alternative to nursing homes? Don't count on it.

Without discussing her plans with anyone, Mrs. Berman, a widow, signed an agreement with a retirement community and paid a fee of more than $60,000. Less than two years later, when her health declined, she received notice that she had to leave within 30 days. The reason they gave was, "your physical and mental condition fails to meet the standards set by the Corporation." Now, more than a year later, they are still holding her money, plus a "service fee" of $600 and a "room preparation fee" of $5,900 for cleaning up her spotless apartment after she left.

Mrs. Berman's dream has turned into a nightmare that thousands of older Americans are experiencing.

She was enticed by the promised security of a "life care" or "continuing care retirement community" (CCRC).

In theory, the idea of continuing care is terrific. The tenant signs a contract and pays an "entrance fee" which buys a life-time residency in the facility. A monthly fee provides for services such as meals, housekeeping, laundry and nursing care, if needed.

Unfortunately, these agreements can be a minefield of problems. According to the contract Mrs. Berman signed, the facility does indeed have the right to terminate the contract on the basis of her health, and put her out within 30 days.

To add insult to injury, upon cancellation the facility may keep a substantial portion of her money as determined by a complicated formula spelled out in her contract. Another blow: they don't have to refund any of her money until her unit has been "resold" to a new occupant. The service fee and room preparation charge? They're legal too — it's all in the contract!

A warning to all those considering entering a Continuing Care Retirement Community: An agreement with a CCRC is a binding legal contract involving your security and a lot of your hard-earned money. Have it reviewed by your lawyer or financial advisor. You both might profit from reading the ABA Checklist for Analyzing CCRC Contracts available from the Commission on Legal Problems of the Elderly, 1800 M Street, N.W., Washington, D.C. 20036

Of course, not all of these facilities are bad. If you are considering a CCRC, check to see if it is accredited by the industry's self-regulatory body, the American Association of Homes for the Aging (AAHA), 1050 17th Street, Washington, D.C., 20036.

Where else can you turn?

Contrary to popular belief, nursing homes are not places that families choose as their first option; they are a last resort. Families will struggle for years to keep their parents or relatives out of a nursing home.

With few exceptions, such as a stroke or an accident, most conditions that incapacitate people start slowly and run their downhill course over a period of years. At the beginning, it is easy for a family to overlook the financial impact of providing care at some future date when the sick person's health has deteriorated. Family members tend to hope that they will somehow be able to manage at home.

Unfortunately, best intentions notwithstanding, people underestimate the physical, emotional, and logistical burdens created by trying to cope with a person who is seriously ill. If they do recognize these problems, the family often assumes that a hospital will be a resource when the time comes that they cannot handle the burdens.

That is no longer the case. Here's why:

Hospitals — Not anymore!

Hospitals have historically been paid through one of four sources:

- Cash
- Medicare
- Medicaid
- Private insurance (such as HMOs and Blue Cross/Blue Shield)

Cash A hospital stay in most metropolitan areas can cost up to $1,000 or more a day depending upon type of care.

Medicare Medicare should not be confused with Medicaid. Medicare is the primary insurance plan that covers people on Social Security. It pays for hospital and medical expenses. The vast majority of older people in hospitals are covered by Medicare.

Prior to 1984, Medicare paid whatever bills were submitted by the hospital for a person's care. The expense to the federal government was so enormous that in 1984 the system was drastically reformed. The federal government established a reimbursement system called Diagnosis Related Groupings (DRGs). Under this system, Medicare pays the hospital a flat rate for a person's illness. If the hospital can stabilize the patient for a cost that is less than what Medicare pays, they keep the change. On the other hand, if the patient cannot be stabilized for the designated amount, the hospital usually pays the additional costs out-of-pocket. Therefore, there is a strong economic incentive for a hospital to move a patient out as soon as he is stabilized.

As a result the word "stabilized" has a much different meaning today than it did prior to 1984. In the old days, a person could stay in the hospital almost indefinitely, until he either got significantly better or died. Today, stabilized does not mean that the patient has gotten better at all. It means that the hospital has determined that the illness won't get any worse.

A man was shocked at the treatment his mother received from a hospital. His mother had suffered a stroke and it was apparent to her son that she was still gravely ill. He felt that the hospital should keep her until she was "stabilized" and ready to go home. The hospital said she had to go. It was the hospital's opinion that she would not have another stroke and by their definition, she was "stabilized" and ready to be discharged.

Under the law, the hospital had the right to discharge his mother. She was discharged in a semi-conscious state, on a catheter, and with a feeding tube going into her stomach.

The remaining two possible methods of payment are Medicaid and private insurance.

Medicaid   This health care system is funded by both the state and federal government. It is only available to the financially needy. Unlike Medicare, there are no deductibles. It pays when nothing else will.

Private insurance (such as HMOs and Blue Cross/Blue Shield)   There are numerous health care plans which people can buy or which are provided by employers to pay for hospital care.

Most private insurers now have a form of DRGs that they use to limit costs.

Taking home a chronically ill person

Regardless of who pays for the hospital, one thing is certain—hospitals are no longer places to get better. Once the patient is stabilized, the family must quickly find another place to care for him. At that point, there are usually only two options left: take the sick person home or put him in a nursing home.

When the sick person's illness or disability takes a mild form, home care may be a viable option for a while. But what happens when he cannot feed or clothe himself or take care of bodily functions without assistance? What if he is incontinent, in pain, depressed, unruly, or hostile? What happens when he cannot be left alone during waking hours? When he must be lifted from a bed to a wheelchair to the toilet and back?

What about the daughter who can't leave the house for twenty minutes because her mother might fall or set the house on fire? There is a saying about dealing with chronically ill people at home: Dealing with someone who is chronically ill eventually makes healthy people chronically ill. The care giver becomes a virtual prisoner in the house. The world closes down. Life as it was before the illness is gone completely.

And who is the care giver? The burdens of caring for our aging population fall disproportionately on women. It is usually the wife, daughter or daughter-in-law who sacrifices her way of life to take care of the chronically ill family member. Often she has sole responsibility in this difficult task. Her life takes a back seat to the needs of the sick person who requires care twenty-four hours a day. She may quit a job and give up all her other activities outside the home. The stress on her is enormous.

The situation affects members of the family not directly responsible for giving care. Families have been known to fall apart over taking care of mother or father. Some marriages are driven to the brink of divorce by the tremendous pressure of coping with the problem.

While the ideal of caring for an incapacitated family member at home is what every loving family aspires to, the realities of the situation are often so difficult that no amount of love, sacrifice, or denial can make it work.

What is left is the last viable, though often least desired, alternative: placement in a nursing home.

The nursing home

Nursing homes provide basically three types of care. They are:

• Medically necessary care (which in many ways approximates hospital care) for which Medicare will pay for a period of time.

• Skilled nursing care which provides patients with continuous care and assistance by nurses and other medical professionals.

• Intermediate care for those who need help with everyday routine activities.

Medicare or other types of medical insurance plans will not pay for skilled nursing care or intermediate care since they are considered custodial care. The yearly cost for this kind of care can run as high as $60,000 in the Northeast and West Coast to $25,000 in the South, Southwest and Midwest. Many people have the mistaken idea that there exists some system or institution which will pay these bills.

People sometimes assume that the Veterans' Administration will pay for veterans who need custodial care. The VA rarely pays unless care is required because of a service-related illness or injury.

So how do people manage when confronted by an overwhelmingly confusing financial dilemma?

Who pays — How the system works

Few people want to escape reasonable financial responsibility for unfortunate circumstances in their own lives. Most people are more than willing to pay their fair share. But in every situation, there comes a point when enough is enough. The central issue in preserving a family's well being is the ability to have a measure of control when a catastrophic illness hits. Make no mistake about it: If families do not take steps early on to protect their assets from the consequences of a long-term illness, they *will* lose control. When that happens, there may be little or nothing left to provide for the surviving spouse and their offspring.

So we go back again to the question: Who pays for long-term nursing home care?

The answer is shocking.

- Private health insurance companies, such as Blue Cross/Blue Shield, will not pay for custodial care.
- The Veterans' Administration, in most cases, will not pay.

- Health Maintenance Organizations (HMOs) or similar insurance plans will not pay.
- Medicare will not pay.

In fact, there are *only three* sources to pay for long-term nursing home care:

- Cash
- Medicaid
- Nursing home insurance

Cash   At a national average cost of nearly $30,000 a year for nursing home care, studies have shown that the average family's life savings will be wiped out in a matter of weeks or months.

Medicaid   No one likes to apply for public assistance. It is one of the great ironies that the very system that older Americans have struggled for years to avoid, for many will be the only means to pay for nursing home care.

Nursing home insurance   Insurance companies are beginning to offer plans that will pay certain amounts towards daily custodial care for a period of years. These policies may be the right answer for those who fear the financial consequences of nursing home confinement but want to maintain control for as long as possible.

If you understand how these systems work, your life savings need not be wiped out. It *is* possible to protect your savings for a surviving spouse or to take care of your children should they need assistance in the future.

It's time to get educated. Let's look at the law and see how the law looks at your assets.

Because the federal government allows each state a certain amount of flexibility in applying the law, the following information by nature must state only general principles. Be sure to refer to the tables to see how your state interprets the regulations. Also, regulations change constantly. Be sure to call your local Department of Public Welfare to see if the rules have changed.

The earlier you begin to plan, the better.

THE BASICS – UNDERSTANDING MEDICAID

Assets

Under the current system, there are two factors that determine eligibility for public assistance: assets and income.

Assets: Definition — everything you own that has value.

That definition seems simple enough. Medicaid, however, divides assets into three categories. Don't try to make sense out of why a particular asset falls into one category and not another. No one ever said that the Medicaid program was rational. In fact, it sometimes appears that Medicaid is as confused as we are in trying to figure out what they will take and what they will let us keep.

The three groups of assets are: countable, non-countable and inaccessible.

Countable assets

Countable assets (also called non-exempt assets)   These are things that Medicaid wants you to spend to zero before financial assistance is available.

They include:

- Cash over $2,000 (in most states)
- Stocks
- Bonds
- IRAs
- Keoghs
- Certificates of deposit
- Single premium deferred annuities
- Treasury notes and treasury bills
- Savings bonds
- Investment property
- Whole life insurance above a certain amount
- Vacation homes
- Second vehicles
- Every other asset that is not specifically listed as non-countable is included in this list

These are things that are in jeopardy when catastrophic illness strikes. In order to qualify for Medicaid the applicant must in effect be BANKRUPT.

Non-countable assets

Non-countable assets (also called exempt assets)
Believe it or not, these things can be worth hundreds

of thousands of dollars but Medicaid has chosen not to count them in determining eligibility. These assets are not in immediate jeopardy.

They include:

- A house used as a primary residence (in most states this includes two- and three-family homes)
- An amount of cash (usually $2,000) (see chart 6 page 246)
- A car
- Personal jewelry
- Household effects
- A pre-paid funeral
- A burial account (not to exceed $2,500 in most states)
- Term life insurance policies (as opposed to whole life) which have no cash surrender value (see chart 8 page 250 for whole life policy limitations)

See chart 8 on page 250 to determine what assets your state allows you to keep.

Life insurance is generally divided into two groups: whole life and term. Whole life has a cash value which increases the longer you hold the policy. Although the insurance lapses when you stop paying, you receive cash value back. This is called the policy's surrender value.

Term insurance never builds up a cash value, but pays a set amount when you die. Coverage stops when you stop paying. Most states allow you to keep unlimited term insurance when applying for Medicaid but only a limited amount of whole life insurance (see chart 8 page 250).

Inaccessible assets

Inaccessible assets – These are countable assets which have been made unavailable to Medicaid. To put it bluntly, *if you can't get them, they can't get them.*

Assets are made inaccessible by

1) Giving them away

2) Holding them in Medicaid trusts (see below)

3) Holding them in certain types of joint accounts (see page 123)

4) An involuntary situation where the person who owns the assets is too incapacitated to get access to them (see page 136)

Medicaid trusts

Holding assets in Medicaid trusts There are two kinds of trusts to consider: revocable and irrevocable. The difference between the two is that the first can be changed after it is set up, the second can't.

A **revocable trust** is a legal instrument that you set up to hold assets. There must be at least one trustee and one or more beneficiaries. A trustee is simply the person who makes the decisions for the trust. The beneficiary is the person who gets the benefit of the assets in the trust. Since you make the trust, you make the rules that the trustee must follow. If you don't like the trust, you can change it or do away with it. That's why it is called revocable. A revocable trust also acts as a will. The rules you make can include who gets your money and under what conditions after you die. While you are alive you receive the benefits. This kind of trust is useful in protecting your house (see Chapter 7), but it will *not* protect countable assets.

An **irrevocable trust**, like a revocable trust, is a legal instrument that you set up to hold assets. Like a revocable trust, there must be one or more trustees and one or more beneficiaries. The definition of a trustee and beneficiary are the same as above. You can make the same rules. The difference is that once you've made the rules you can't change them. By making it irrevocable you give up the power to modify or do away with the trust. Simply put, you lose control.

The only trust that will protect countable assets is an irrevocable trust but *only* one that limits the amount of discretion a trustee has. These are called **Medicaid Trusts.**

Congress passed a law that took effect in 1986 restricting the use of irrevocable trusts. It says that if you set up an irrevocable trust, name yourself as a beneficiary, and give power to your trustee to give you all, some or none of the income and assets, Medicaid will assume your trustee will make all the income and principal available to you and thus the nursing home. It doesn't matter that your trustee can say, "I have the power to refuse to give the nursing home any money." Medicaid won't buy it.

The trust has to be set up in such a way as to limit the power of the trustee. If, for example, the trustee has no power to give you the assets, but only to hold them, Medicaid can't get them. It's the old principle, "If I can't get them, you can't get them."

Example: **An irrevocable trust that *doesn't* protect assets**

A husband and wife set up The ABC Family Trust. They name their son as the trustee and themselves as beneficiaries. They give the trustee the power to give them all, some or none of the principal and income. The day a parent/beneficiary goes into the nursing home is the day the "snapshot"* is taken of the couple's assets. Since they gave discretion over the assets and income to the trustee, Medicaid assumes that the trustee will use his full discretion and make the assets and income available to the parent. In other words, the assets are considered countable, available, and therefore subject to division just as if they weren't in trust.

* For a detailed explanation of "snapshots" and how Medicaid treats assets held by spouses, see page 55.

A typical effective trust gives the trustee no discretion over principal but allows him/her to distribute income from the principal to the beneficiaries. Unfortunately, that money could end up going to the nursing home. Here's what you could do:

Example: An irrevocable trust that *does* protect assets

A husband and wife set up The ABC Family Trust with the same trustee and beneficiaries as in the previous example. This time they don't give any power to the trustee to give them the assets, only the power to hold them in trust while they generate income. The day a parent goes into the nursing home is the day the snapshot is taken of their assets. However, this time the assets in the trust are not in the snapshot because the trustee cannot make them available to the parent.

The income can go to either or both spouses and the principal is 100 percent protected. In the example above, the income can be made payable to either or both beneficiaries in any amount that you wish. For example, if the husband is sick, the wife can set up the irrevocable trust to hold the assets and receive the income, providing 30 months have passed before applying for Medicaid. None of the income would go to the nursing home. If both spouses are healthy at the time the trust is set up, a provision can be made to divide the income – which means you risk only half if one goes in. Further, you might be able to put in a provision to discontinue income payments to an ill spouse giving income only to the healthy one.

If you find the prospect of never again being able to get at your principal hard to accept, there is an alternative you may want to explore. The beneficiaries (the husband and wife or single person who established the trust) name another person (a trusted son or daughter, perhaps) as the beneficiary along with themselves. The trustee has discretion to give principal to that other beneficiary. That beneficiary can then make a gift of the money to the person who set up the trust.

Putting aside the issue of trust, there is a distinct possibility that Medicaid will challenge this last arrangement because the intent is so obvious.

WARNING: There are thousands of Medicaid qualifying trusts that were set up prior to 1986 which were made invalid by the law Congress passed that year. Today, none of these trusts will protect assets even though they were legal and effective when set up. If your trust was established before 1986, be sure to contact your attorney to make the appropriate changes. Any changes you make, will not be retroactive, but will again start the 30-month clock (see page 114) from the date the changes are made.

REMEMBER: In defining non-countable assets, specifics vary from state to state. Be sure to check chart 8 on page 250 to see how assets are classified in your locale. Also, regulations change, so be sure to check with your local welfare agency when planning or filling out an application for Medicaid.

The Spousal Impoverishment Act

The Spousal Impoverishment Act (SIA) which Congress passed in 1988 supposedly protects a stay-at-home spouse (the person not going into the nursing home) by allowing him or her to keep certain amounts of assets and income.

As of October 1, 1989, Medicaid treats marital assets this way:

Step 1 — Medicaid fixes the day a spouse goes into a nursing home or medical institution.

Step 2 — Medicaid requires that the couple list all their countable assets regardless of whose name they are in, who earned them or how long they've been in either's name, including any assets that were transferred within the past 30 months.

Step 3 — Medicaid takes a snapshot, a picture of the combined assets on the day the spouse goes into the nursing home or medical institution.

Step 4 — The stay-at-home spouse is then allowed to keep one-half of the total amount of the assets in the snapshot, but **not less than $13,296 or more than $66,480.** (This figure will continue to go up annually.)

Example: Curtis is going into a nursing home on June 1. He and his wife Helen have total assets of $20,000, $15,000 of which is in his IRA. Medicaid will take a snapshot of the couple's combined assets on June 1. Helen will be allowed to keep one-half of $20,000. Since half of $20,000 is $10,000, she will be allowed to keep $13,296, the minimum.

If Curtis and Helen had $150,000, Helen would not be allowed to keep half ($75,000) but only $66,480, the maximum.

To make matters a little more confusing, although the principles here are consistent across the board, the dollar amounts may vary from state to state. The law allows each state to set the amount the stay-at-home spouse may keep between a minimum of

$13,296 and a maximum of $66,480. Here's how that works:

Your state may decide to raise the floor on the amount a stay-at-home spouse may keep of the couple's joint assets. Rather than a floor of $13,296, your state may allow $40,000. What happens in our example when the floor is raised to $40,000? Helen would be allowed to keep the entire $20,000 because her state raised the floor from $13,296 to $40,000 (see chart 1 page 241).

An application for Medicaid is usually not made on the day the spouse goes into the nursing home, unless, of course, their assets are so low that they already qualify for Medicaid. Whether he or she will be able to qualify is determined by using the method described on page 58.

If assets must be spent down by the institutionalized spouse in order to qualify, the application for Medicaid may not take place for months. Regardless of what the total assets are on the day he applies, the stay-at-home spouse's share will always be determined on the day of the snapshot, admission day to a hospital for at least 30 days or to a nursing home.

Example: Joel and Esther have combined countable assets of $100,000 when Esther goes into a nursing home on January 1. The snapshot is taken on that day. Joel's spousal share (the amount he is allowed to keep) is $50,000. Unless Esther buys non-countable assets or otherwise protects her money (see page 47), she will have to spend $48,000 on her care ($50,000 minus $2,000, the maximum assets she can keep).

Let's say that Joel applies for Medicaid for his wife when there is $70,000 left of countable assets. All Esther would have to spend is $18,000. Why? Because Medicaid goes back to January 1 to determine Joel's share ($50,000). This amount deducted from $70,000 leaves $20,000 that Esther will have to spend. She is allowed to keep $2,000 of that amount.

You may be confused in thinking that in taking the snapshot, you are applying for Medicaid. That's not the case unless the snapshot reveals that your assets are less than the maximum limit to qualify for Medicaid. If the assets exceed these amounts, you must then spend down to the limits set by your state (see chart 1 on page 241).

Income

Definition — Income is all the money you receive from any source. Like countable assets, it is in jeopardy.

The money may come from one or a combination of the following:

- Social security
- Interest and investments
- Trusts
- Rental units
- Help from family members
- Pensions
- Annuities
- In a nutshell, you name it, if you get it, Medicaid wants it

Income eligibility is quite simple. In most states, if the person who is going into the nursing home has monthly income that exceeds the nursing home bill, he pays the nursing home directly. (See charts 2 and 3 pages 242, 243 showing what states set limits on monthly income.) Also see page 145 for a discussion of "cap states."

If that person's monthly income is less than the

nursing home bill, Medicaid has him give it to the home and Medicaid makes up the difference. Most, if not all, of your income, regardless of where it comes from, for whatever reason you get it, will have to go to the nursing home.

Most states allow a person to keep:

- a personal needs allowance (see chart 4 page 244)
- a home maintenance allowance if planning to go home
- a monthly premium to pay for medical insurance

Income rules do not apply to the stay-at-home spouse. She is free to continue working and keep all her salary and other monthly income (like social security). In addition, the state usually allows the spouse to keep her half of the assets that generate income such as dividends, rent, etc.

The law requires states to set a specified amount the stay-at-home spouse may keep from total joint income. As of September 1991, the minimum is $856 per month, the maximum $1,662. The states have discretion in setting the amount within those limits. The well spouse has the opportunity to increase the state-set amount if she can show that her housing expenses are unusually high.

Example: Dennis' and Eleanor's only income is $1,200 a month in social security. Of that, $1,000 is the husband's, $200 is his wife's. If Dennis goes into a nursing home he will be allowed to make the following deductions from his $1,000:

- *a personal needs account (approximately $50 a month in most states. See chart 4 page 244)*
- *the premium for his medex or equivalent insurance policy that pays the deductibles on his Medicare policy*
- *$656 monthly to supplement his wife's $200 a month since the minimum she is provided from the spousal income is $856*

Remember, Eleanor's income is unaffected. If she is working, she can keep her entire salary. She does not have to make a contribution to Dennis' nursing home expense.

HOW TO PROTECT ASSETS WHEN THERE IS TIME TO PLAN

When a diagnosis is made early and the illness is expected to progress slowly, the family has time to plan. This is the time to start protecting assets. The key to protection is knowing what assets and income are in jeopardy and what the critical deadlines are for transferring them. In the preceding chapter, we identified which assets and income are in jeopardy.

Our goal is to take countable assets (those that have to be spent to zero) (see page 46), and make them either non-countable, and therefore protected (see page 47), or inaccessible which means that Medicaid can't get them (see page 49). In the following chapter, we will look at the options available to people in different situations.

Remember: The key to protecting assets when you have time to plan is understanding the rules about disqualification.

The Disqualification Period – 30 months

When a transfer of a countable asset is made to the inaccessible category (see page 49), the person making the transfer is disqualified for a period of months. Read and memorize the following rule:

If you transfer countable assets for less than fair market value within 30 months of applying for Medicaid, it is presumed that you did it to have Medicaid pay the expense of institutional care.

Example: Sam transfers all his savings ($50,000) to his son on January 1,1991. He goes into a nursing home on January 1, 1992. Since he gave his money away within 30 months of being institutionalized, he will not qualify for Medicaid until either 18 months have passed (30 months minus the 12 months that passed between the date of transfer and his entry into the home) or until he has used up on nursing home bills all the transferred money.

The exceptions to this are covered in Chapter 5. Please note that if the person went into a nursing home before October 1, 1989, in most states he would be covered by the state's old laws. Disqualification periods prior to that date ran from two to five years depending on what state you were in. In October 1989 the disqualification period was set at 30 months for all states.

Since he would be under his state's old law, there may be severe penalties for applying for Medicaid within the old disqualification time. Never apply for Medicaid benefits until after the entire disqualification period (old and new) has passed.

At this point we have covered the general principles involved in protecting assets. Now let's get down to specifics.

Understanding the law

The law *prior* to November, 1989: A good example of how fast Medicaid law is changing is the November 1989 revision of the regulation covering spousal transfer of assets. Prior to that time, the only spouse prohibited from transferring assets was the one being institutionalized. As long as the stay-at-home spouse had countable assets in her name for at least 30 months, she was free to transfer them without penalty even if the transfer occurred the day before the snapshot.

The law *after* November, 1989: Even if the stay-at-home spouse has had all the countable assets in her name alone for at least 30 months when her husband goes into a nursing home, under the new law, if she tries to transfer the assets to her children, Medicaid will consider the transfer as if her husband had made it: He will be disqualified for 30 months or until the countable assets are spent.

The option of giving all the countable assets to the healthy spouse for the purpose of protecting them from Medicaid is no longer viable.

At this point we have covered the general principles involved in protecting assets. Now let's get down to specifics.

There is no single course of action that best suits every situation. To demonstrate the various options, we will explore several examples. One of these will closely fit your own situation. The examples cover asset protection for:

- Spouses
- Offspring and parents
- Offspring and single parent
- Siblings
- Nieces/nephews and aunts/uncles
- Grandchildren and grandparents
- Unrelated people

In each example, we will consider the pros and cons of all the options available in these particular circumstances. After reviewing the choices, we will determine which option best suits the needs of the people involved.

All examples assume that the family has at least 30 months before nursing home confinement.

Spouses

This example deals with a spouse who may need nursing home care in the future (at least 30 months) and how his family can help protect the family's assets. The Andrews have a close and trusting relationship with daughter Susan, but not with son Bill.

NAME:	Mr. and Mrs. Andrews
AGE:	husband 65
	wife 65
ASSETS:	house $150,000 (jointly held, no mortgage)
	savings (joint) $48,000
	(includes wife's inheritance of $10,000)
INSURANCE:	husband has two insurance policies, a whole life policy with a face value of $10,000 and a cash surrender value of $2,000, and a term policy worth $25,000.
INCOME:	from joint savings $4,000/year
	social security: husband $650/month
	wife $300/month
HEALTH:	husband, early Alzheimer's
	wife, good
FAMILY:	two adult children, Bill and Susan

The goal is to take countable assets and move them to the non-countable or inaccessible column. Here is how the assets would be categorized at the time of the Alzheimer's diagnosis before steps are taken to protect them:

non-countable	countable	inaccessible
house	joint savings	none presently
term policy	$48,000	
	whole life insurance policy $2,000 CSV	

* The state in which the Andrews live considers the entire cash surrender value (CSV) to be a countable asset. (see chart 8 for your state limits.)

What happens when the husband and wife don't plan

If assets remain in the countable column, they will have to be spent on nursing home care, subject to the Spousal Impoverishment Act (see page 55), before the husband qualifies for financial assistance. If the husband transfers the assets to the inaccessible column within 30 months of going into a nursing home, Medicaid presumes that he is trying to hide the assets and he will be denied assistance.

Here's what will happen if the assets remain exactly as they appear above:

On the day the husband goes into the nursing home, Medicaid will take a snapshot (see page 55) of the couple's assets regardless of whose name they are in. Since the countable assets were not shifted to other categories, the wife will be allowed to keep only a specified amount. That figure is arrived at by applying a somewhat confusing formula: She may keep no less than $13,296 OR one half of their combined total assets up to a limit of $66,480, whichever is greater.

Looking at the Andrews chart, we see that their joint funds including the cash surrender value of their life insurance policy are $50,000. Half of that is $25,000. Since $25,000 is greater than $13,296 and less than $66,480 she is allowed to keep $25,000.

Here's what happens if their savings account is $15,000 instead of $50,000. One half of $15,000 is $7,500. Because $7,500 is less than $13,296, she gets to keep the greater amount ($13,296) since that's the *minimum* the law allows.

What would have happened if their savings account had been $200,000? One half is $100,000. Because $100,000 is greater than $66,480, she gets to keep only $66,480 since that is the *maximum* the law allows.

If you are feeling confused, there's nothing wrong with you. This concept can be difficult to grasp. Go back and read the example again.

Individual states are allowed by law to raise the amount the stay-at-home spouse may keep (see chart 1 page 241).

What happens if the state where the Andrews live raises to $40,000 the minimum amount that the stay-at-home spouse could keep? Our chart shows total countable assets of $50,000. One half of $50,000 is $25,000. Because the floor is now $40,000, the wife in our example gets to keep not one half or $25,000 but $40,000 of their $50,000 in joint assets.

Now, let's say that the couple had $150,000 in joint assets. One half is $75,000. Because $75,000 is more than the ceiling of $66,480, she would keep only

$66,480. In this case, the floor ($40,000) is not used.

What happens when the husband and wife have time to plan

Let's look at the various options we might use to protect those assets if the Andrews have 30 months or more before nursing home confinement.

Remember: Assets may be protected (made inaccessible) by

Option 1 Giving them away
      A – One spouse to the other
      B – To the offspring

Option 2 Holding them in trust
Option 3 Holding them in certain types of joint accounts
Option 4 An involuntary situation where the applicant is too sick to gain access (not applicable in the Andrews' situation)

After examining each option, we will see which is best suited for this specific situation.

Option 1A Giving away assets — One spouse to the other

Prior to November 1989, Mr. Andrews could have taken his name and social security number off all the countable assets. They would then be in the name of his wife only, or if she wished, she could add a son or daughter as a co-holder.

Let's say thirty months had passed from the day of the transfer. Under the old law, if Mr. Andrews were institutionalized, his wife would have been free to transfer the assets to the children as long as it was done before the day of the snapshot. Since the wife was not being institutionalized, her assets (those in her name for at least 30 months) could be transferred without penalty.

If Mr Andrews were institutionalized anytime after November, 1989, the new law would apply. Let's say Mrs. Andrews has had all the countable assets in her name alone for at least 30 months. Her husband is going into a nursing home tomorrow. Under the new law, if she tries to transfer the assets to her children, Medicaid will consider the transfer as if her husband had made it: He will be disqualified for 30 months or until the countable assets are spent.

Option 1B   Giving away assets – To the offspring

Here's a little wisdom to ponder: Never give your assets to your children unless you are absolutely, positively willing to stake your life on the belief that they will give them back or make them available to you when you ask.

Here's what you want to avoid:

• The children spending your money because they "thought it was a gift"

• Your son's or daughter's spouse (whom you never liked in the first place) getting your assets in a divorce

• Your son or daughter losing the money in a bad business deal

A rule of thumb in determining whether your offspring should be the choice to hold and protect your assets: If you have to think more than one half of one second before you answer "yes," forget the whole idea. On the other hand, if you do have a close and trusting relationship with your offspring, you can enlist their help in protecting your assets.

Option 2   Holding assets in trust

There are different kinds of trusts to consider. For a complete explanation, before continuing please go back and read pages 50-54.

Example: An irrevocable trust that *doesn't* protect assets

The Andrews set up The Andrews Family Trust naming their children as trustees and themselves as beneficiaries. They give the trustees the power to give them all or some or none of the principal and income. The day Mr. Andrews goes into the nursing home is the day a snapshot is taken of their assets (see page 55). Since they gave discretion over the assets and income to the trustees, Medicaid assumes that the trustees will use their power and make the assets and income available to the parents. In other words, the assets are considered countable and therefore available, subject to the Spousal Impoverishment Act (see page 55).

Example: An irrevocable trust that *does* protect assets

The Andrews set up The Andrews Family Trust with their children as trustees and themselves as beneficiaries. This time, however, they don't give any power to the trustees to give them the assets, only the power to hold them in trust while they generate income for the parents. The day Mr. Andrews goes into the nursing home is the day the snapshot is taken of their assets. However, this time the assets in the trust are not in the snapshot because the trustees cannot make them available to their parents. However, Medicaid may get the income (see chapter 6).

Here's what the Andrews can do to protect their assets:

Plan A   Establish an irrevocable trust like the second example above; OR

Plan B   Establish an irrevocable trust like the second example above but naming a third person as a beneficiary and giving the trustee power to distribute funds to that third person.

The Andrews establish the Andrews Family Trust, making it irrevocable. They name themselves as beneficiaries along with a third person, such as their daughter Susan. They name a fourth party as trustee and give him control over the assets. The trust allows the trustee to give only Susan the principal at any time, never Mr. and Mrs. Andrews. The Andrews can only get money through Susan, the third beneficiary. If either of the Andrews goes into a nursing home, the principal will be protected since the trustee never had discretion to give principal to either of them.

Plan C   Establish a revocable trust naming Mr. and Mrs. Andrews as beneficiaries but specifying that the trust becomes irrevocable if either one of them goes into a nursing home or has a long-term illness.

Consider the options:

Plan A means that the Andrews give up full control of the assets well before the husband goes into the home. This is the same as giving them away. Also, they can't get their principal.

Plan B also means that the Andrews give up full control of their assets. However, they can still get their principal because the trustee can give the assets to a third person who in turn could make them available to the Andrews.

During the time that the Andrews are not in a nursing home, they will have to get their assets through that third party (such as a son or daughter or close friend).

If Mr. Andrews goes into a home, the trustee can still get money to Mrs. Andrews by using the above method.

However you slice it though, this trust takes control away from the Andrews. If the Andrews do not feel comfortable with giving this power to a relative or close friend, this option doesn't work for them.

Plan C means that the Andrews' assets are countable and available to Medicaid for 30 months. Why? Because revocable trusts don't protect countable assets.

The trust in Plan C only becomes irrevocable when there's a long-term illness or nursing home confinement. Therefore 30 months must expire before the assets are protected. This plan is useful only for people with a great deal of money who can easily afford to pay privately for 30 months. The Andrews can't.

Which plan is best?

If a trust is to be used, Plan B is best because it

protects the assets while still making them available through a third person. The key is that the third person must be trustworthy.

Option 3   Holding assets in a joint account

The Andrews, like most couples, hold their assets in an "either/or" savings account. "Either" the husband "or" the wife can gain access to the account without the other's signature. Medicaid considers this type of account available when determining countable assets.

There's another type of account that the Andrews could open that requires both signatures. This is called an "and" account because both his "and" her signatures are required for either one to get the money.

In some states (be sure to check with your Department of Public Welfare), an "and" account is protected from being spent on a chronic care facility or nursing home if the stay-at-home spouse refuses to co-sign the check or withdrawal slip to give the ill spouse access to the account. It remains inaccessible until the spouse in the nursing home dies. At that time the funds belong to the survivor, free and clear.

If the Andrews have a savings account that requires two signatures, Mrs. Andrews can make the entire amount inaccessible by simply refusing to co-sign the withdrawal slip.

Drawbacks:

1) If Mrs. Andrews dies while her husband is in the nursing home, the entire balance becomes available to the nursing home. If he is on Medicaid, he will immediately be disqualified because he now has money.

2) Although the money is frozen until Mr. Andrews dies, it also is unavailable to Mrs. Andrews. Why? Because Mrs. Andrews needs her husband's signature to take money from the account. Any withdrawal would immediately be considered countable and available to pay the nursing home. (Medicaid would find out about the transfer since most states request a periodic update from the applicant. Since Mr. Andrews declared this account on his application, Medicaid would be on the lookout for any changes in status.)

The above option of holding money in an "and" account is not practical if you have 30 months or more to plan. It can be useful when you are in a crisis situation (see page 123).

Life Insurance   In reviewing how the Andrews'
assets are divided, you will notice that his term
policy is non-countable and therefore can be kept.
Not so with his whole life policy since the face
value, not the cash surrender value, exceeds a
certain face amount (see chart 8 page 250). Mr.
Andrews could transfer ownership of the policy or
one of the children to make it inaccessible.

WHICH OF OUR OPTIONS IS BEST?

Option 2, Plan B – holding money with a third
person as beneficiary, is the best alternative other
than giving the money outright to the Andrews'
children.

Here is how the transferred assets line up:

non-countable	countable	inaccessible
house term policy	0	whole life insurance policy now owned by Susan. Assets in irrevocable trust

A note about the Andrews' house:

It makes no sense to protect the Andrews' money without protecting the house too. Even though it is a non-countable asset (Medicaid allows the Andrews to keep it while receiving financial assistance), they will place a lien on the house upon the death of both spouses. Please refer to chapter 7 for a complete explanation of how to protect a house.

Offspring and parents

This example deals with elderly parents who are both in frail health. The Rossis have a close and trusting relationship with their children; therefore the children are available to help their parents protect their assets.

NAME:	Mr. and Mrs. Rossi	
CHILDREN:	Maria and Joseph	
PARENTS' AGES:	husband, 82, wife, 79	
ASSETS:	two-family house,	$150,000
	savings bonds	$25,000
	stocks	$30,000
	savings and CDs	$45,000
INCOME:	husband	$600/month social security, $500/month pension
	wife	$250 /month social security, $150/month pension
	joint	$350/month investment interest
HEALTH:	husband	Parkinson's disease, early stage
	wife	fair

Our goal is to protect countable assets from being spent on Mr. Rossi's expected nursing home confinement.

Before continuing, go back to page 55 and review the Spousal Impoverishment Act.

Here's how the assets line up before steps are taken to protect them:

non-countable	countable	inaccessible
2-family house	savings and CDs $45,000	none presently
	stocks $30,000	
	savings bonds $25,000	

What happens when the family has time to plan

Let's look at the various options to protect assets when Mr. Rossi has 30 months or more before nursing home confinement.

Remember, assets may be protected (made inaccessible) by:

Option 1 Giving away assets

A – One spouse to the other
B – To the offspring

Option 2   Holding them in trust

Option 3   Holding them in certain types of
            joint accounts

Option 4   **An involuntary situation where the
            applicant is too sick to gain access**
            (not applicable in the Rossis' case)

After examining each option, we will see which is best suited for this specific situation.

Option 1A   Giving away assets — One spouse to the other

This option makes little sense in the Rossis' situation because neither of them is in good health.

Option 1B   Giving away assets — To the offspring

Since the Rossis have a close relationship with Maria and Joseph and trust their judgment, they may choose to transfer all the assets to them. As long as 30 months pass from the date of the transfer, the assets will not be counted in determining

Medicaid eligibility for Mr. Rossi.

Drawbacks

1) Either or both of the Rossi children may get a divorce. Most states would consider the parents' assets part of the offsprings' marital property subject to division.

2) Maria or Joseph might die, which means that their spouse could inherit the assets being held for their parents.

To avoid these problems, both should sign an agreement with their spouses stating that the assets are being held for their parents and are not part of the marital property. Also, each should make a will specifying that the money they are holding is to be placed in a trust for their parents' use. The trust should state that upon the death of both parents, the assets will be given to whomever the parents wish.

Option 2 – Holding assets in trust

There are different kinds of trusts to consider. For a complete explanation before continuing please go back and read pages 50-54.

Example: An irrevocable trust that <u>doesn't</u> protect assets

The husband and wife set up The Rossi Family Trust. They name their son and daughter as trustees and themselves as beneficiaries. They give the trustees the power to give them all, some or none of the principal and income. The day Mr. Rossi goes into the nursing home is the day the snapshot (see page 55) is taken of the couple's assets. Since they gave discretion over the assets and income to the trustees, Medicaid assumes that the trustees will use their discretion to make the assets and income available to their parents. In other words, the assets are considered countable and therefore available subject to the Spousal Impoverishment Act (see page 55).

Example: An irrevocable trust that <u>does</u> protect assets

Mr. and Mrs. Rossi set up The Rossi Family Trust with the same trustees and beneficiaries. This time, however, they don't give any power to the trustees to give them the assets, only the power to hold assets in trust while they generate income for them. The day Mr. Rossi goes into the nursing home is the day the snapshot is taken of their assets. However, now the assets in the trust are not in the snapshot because the trustees cannot make them available to their parents.

Here's what the Rossis could do to protect their assets:

Plan A   Establish an irrevocable trust like the second example above; OR

Plan B Establish an irrevocable trust naming one of their children as a third beneficiary and giving the trustees power to distribute funds to that person.

During the time that the Rossis are not in a nursing home they will have to get their assets through that third party. If Mr. Rossi goes into a home, the trustee can still get money to Mrs. Rossi by using the above method.

Plan C   Establish a revocable trust naming the Rossis as beneficiaries but specifying that the trust becomes irrevocable if either one of them goes into a nursing home or has a long-term illness.

Which of the above choices is best?

Plan A means that the Rossis give up full control of the assets well before the husband goes into the home. This is the same as giving away assets. It also means that they can't get at their principal.

Plan B still means that the Rossis give up full control of their assets. However, they can still get at their principal because the trustee can give the assets to third parties, such as Maria and/or Joseph. During the time that neither of the Rossis is in a nursing home, the trustee, who has the power to give principal to third parties, gives money to Maria. She, in turn, can make a gift of the money to her parents. If Mr. Rossi goes into a home, the trustee could still get money to Mrs. Rossi by using the above method. However you slice it, though, this trust still takes control away from the Rossis.

Plan C means that the Rossis' assets are countable for 30 months. Why? Because revocable trusts don't protect countable assets. The trust in Plan C only becomes irrevocable when there's a long term illness or nursing home confinement. Therefore 30 months must expire before the assets are protected. This option is useful only for people with a great deal of money who can easily afford to pay privately for 30 months. The Rossis can't.

Plan B is the best choice because the Rossis have a

close and trusting relationship with their offspring. One caution: In some states only one of the children can be the third beneficiary; if both are listed the trust might be invalid. Check the law in the state where you live.

Option 3   Holding assets in joint accounts

The Rossis, like most couples, hold their assets in an "either/or" savings account. "Either" the husband "or" the wife can gain access to the account without the other's signature. Medicaid considers this type of account available when determining countable assets. In other words, one half of the assets would have to be spent on the nursing home.

There's another type of account that the Rossis could open that requires both signatures. This is called an "and" account because both his "and" her signature are required for either one to get the money (see page 123).

In some states (make sure you check with your local Department of Public Welfare), an "and" account is protected from being spent on a nursing home if the stay-at-home spouse refuses to co-sign the check or withdrawal slip to give the ill spouse access to the account. It remains inaccessible until the spouse in the nursing home dies.

In our example, if any of the Rossis' investments required two signatures, Mrs. Rossi could make the entire amount inaccessible by simply refusing to co-sign the withdrawal slip.

Again: Because regulations vary from state to state, be sure to check with your local welfare office to be sure an "and" account is considered inaccessible.

Drawbacks

1) If Mrs. Rossi dies while her husband is in the nursing home, the entire balance will become available to the nursing home. If he was on Medicaid, he will immediately be disqualified because he now has money.

2) Although the money is frozen until Mr. Rossi dies, it also is unavailable to his wife. Why? Because Mrs. Rossi needs her husband's signature to take money out of the account. Any withdrawal would immediately be considered countable and available to the nursing home. (Medicaid would find out about the transfer since most states request periodic updates from the applicant. Since Mr. Rossi

declared this account on his application, Medicaid would be on the lookout for any changes in status.)

Because of these drawbacks and the fact that the Rossis have at least 30 months to plan, the option of holding money in an "and" account is not the best choice for them. (An "and" account can be useful when you are in a crisis situation; see page 123.)

WHICH OF OUR OPTIONS IS BEST?

Either Option 1B, giving away assets — To the offspring or Option 2, Plan B, holding assets in an irrevocable trust with a third beneficiary, would be the best solutions.

Here is how the transferred assets line up:

non-countable	countable	inaccessible
2-family house	0	assets are placed in an irrevocable trust or assets are given outright to offspring

A note about the Rossis' house: It makes no sense to protect the Rossis' money without protecting the house too. Even though it is a non-countable asset (Medicaid allows the Rossis to keep it while receiving financial assistance), a lien will be placed on the house upon the death of both spouses. Please refer to Chapter 7 for a complete explanation of how to protect a house.

Offspring and single parent

This example is used to show how children can help a widowed parent who is too ill to handle her own assets.

NAME:	Mrs. Stein, Mr. Stein deceased
CHILDREN:	one daughter, Ruth (married)
AGE:	86
ASSETS:	savings $75,000
INCOME:	social security $400/month
	investments $500/month
HEALTH:	early stage Alzheimer's

The goal is to protect countable assets from being spent on Mrs. Stein's nursing home confinement.

Here's how the assets line up before steps are taken to protect them:

non-countable	countable	inaccessible
none	$75,000	none presently

If assets remain in the countable column, they will have to be spent on nursing home care before Mrs. Stein qualifies for financial assistance. If these assets are transferred to the inaccessible column within 30 months of going into a nursing home, Medicaid presumes that the transfer was done to hide the assets.

Let's look at the various options we might use to protect those assets if Mrs. Stein has 30 months or more before nursing home confinement.

Remember, assets may be protected (made inaccessible) by:

Option 1 – Giving them away

Option 2 – Holding them in trust

Option 3 – Holding them in certain types of joint accounts

Option 4 – An involuntary situation where the applicant is too sick to gain access
(not applicable in the Steins' situation)

After examining each option, we will see which is best suited for this specific situation.

Option 1 Giving away assets

If her savings account is held jointly with her daughter, Mrs. Stein can simply take off her name and social security number. If the account is in her name alone, the money can be transferred to an account with only her daughter's name and social security number. If Mrs. Stein can stay out of a nursing home for 30 months or more, the money is protected because she is only prohibited from receiving Medicaid benefits if she transfers the money within 30 months of entering the nursing home or applying for assistance.

Drawbacks

1) Ruth may die while holding her mother's money. Ruth can handle this by making a will which sets up a trust for her mother's benefit. She would have to

choose a person to handle the trust (a trustee) and a person(s) who would get the money upon her mother's death.

2) Ruth may get divorced. Most states consider a couple's assets as joint property regardless of whose name is on them. Ruth should set up an agreement with her husband excluding her mother's assets from their joint property. If Ruth is single but is planning to get married, she should sign a pre-marital agreement excluding the assets in the event of a divorce.

Option 2   Holding assets in trust

There are different kinds of trusts to consider. For a complete explanation, before continuing please go back to pages 50-54.

Example: An irrevocable trust that *doesn't* protect assets

Mrs. Stein can set up The Stein Family Trust naming her daughter as trustee and herself as beneficiary. She gives Ruth the power to give her all, some or none of the principal and income. Since she gave discretion over the assets and income to the trustee, Medicaid assumes that the trustee will use her power

*and make the assets and income available to her
mother. In other words, the assets are considered
countable and therefore available (see page 46).*

**Example: An irrevocable trust that *does* protect
assets**

*Mrs. Stein sets up The Stein Family Trust with the
same trustee and beneficiary. This time, however, she
doesn't give any power to the trustee to give her the
assets, only the power to hold them in trust while they
generate income for her. However, this time the
assets in the trust are not available because the
trustee has no authority to give them to her mother.*

Here's what Mrs. Stein could do:

Plan A   Establish an irrevocable trust like the
second example above; OR

Plan B   Establish a revocable trust naming herself
as beneficiary but specifying that the trust becomes
irrevocable if she goes into a nursing home or has a
long-term illness.

Which option is best?

Plan A means that Mrs. Stein gives up full control of
the assets well before she goes into the home. This

is the same as giving assets away.

Plan B means that Mrs. Stein's assets are countable for 30 months because revocable trusts don't protect countable assets. The trust in Plan B only becomes irrevocable when there's a long-term illness or nursing home confinement. Therefore 30 months must expire before the assets are protected. This option is useful only for people with a great deal of money who can easily afford to pay privately for 30 months. Mrs. Stein can't.

If any trust is to be used, Plan A is the best choice because Mrs. Stein has a close and trusting relationship with her daughter.

Option 3   Holding assets in joint accounts

Mrs. Stein, like many widows, holds her assets in an "either/or" account with an offspring, in this case Ruth. Either the mother *or* the daughter can gain access to the account without the other's signature. Medicaid considers this type of account completely owned by Mrs. Stein unless she can prove otherwise. Why? Because the presumption is that the money is really Mrs. Stein's and her daughter's name is on the account for the sake of convenience.

There's another type of account that Mrs. Stein could open that requires both signatures. This is called an "and" account because both hers *"and"* her daughter's signature are required for either one to get the money.

In some states (be sure to check your Department of Public Welfare), an "and" account is protected from being spent on a nursing home if the co-holder refuses to co-sign the check or withdrawal slip to give the ill person access to the account. The account remains inaccessible until the person in the nursing home dies.

In our example, if any of Mrs. Stein's investments required two signatures, Ruth could make the entire amount inaccessible by simply refusing to co-sign the withdrawal slip.

Drawbacks

Money or investments held in an "and" account becomes vulnerable in two situations: First, the money becomes a countable asset to Mrs. Stein if Ruth dies first. Second, even though Ruth will probably outlive her mother, this money may be frozen until her mother dies. Because regulations vary from state to state, be sure to check with your local welfare office to be sure an "and" account is considered inaccessible.

WHICH OF OUR OPTIONS IS BEST?

1) Giving away assets
2) Holding assets in trust
3) Holding assets jointly

Option 1 – giving away assets to her daughter, would be the best approach since mother and daughter have a close relationship and there are no other family members to consider.

Here is how the transferred assets would line up:

non-countable	countable	inaccessible
none	none	all cash given away to daughter

Siblings

This example is used to show the dangers of holding assets jointly with siblings and how one sibling can help the other protect assets.

NAME:	Ethel and Coretta Johnson
AGES:	81 and 77, respectively
ASSETS:	CDs $10,000
	savings $30,000
	2-family house $150,000
	(all above held jointly)
	insurance, whole life,
	cash surrender value $10,000
INCOME:	Ethel's social security $350/month
	Coretta's social security $300/month
	joint, from investments $250/month
HEALTH:	Ethel has been in poor health for years and has a history of heart problems
	Coretta is in good health

The goal is to protect countable assets from being spent on Ethel's nursing home confinement.

Here's how the assets line up:

non-countable	countable	inaccessible
2-family house	$10,000	none presently
	$30,000 savings	
	whole life policy,	
	CVS $10,000	

When siblings have time to plan

If assets remain in the countable column, they will have to be spent on nursing home care before Ethel qualifies for financial assistance (see page 46). If they are transferred to the inaccessible column within 30 months of going into a nursing home, Medicaid presumes that Ethel was trying to hide the assets and she will not qualify for assistance. Let's look at the various options we might use to protect those assets if there will be 30 months or more before nursing home confinement.

Remember, assets may be protected by:

Option 1 – Giving them away
Option 2 – Holding them in trust
Option 3 – Holding them in certain types of
            joint accounts
Option 4 – An involuntary situation where the
            applicant is too sick to gain access to
            countable assets
            (not applicable in
            the Johnson's situation)

After examining each option, we will see which is best suited for this specific situation.

Option 1   Giving away assets

Since the investments are held jointly with her sister, Ethel can simply take off her name and social security number. If the investments were in her name alone, they could be transferred to an account with only her sister's name and social security number.

Since Ethel's insurance policy has a cash surrender value of $10,000 and it would have to be spent to zero before eligibility, she should transfer ownership to her sister. She would remain the insured and her sister would continue to be the beneficiary.

If Ethel can stay out of a nursing home for 30 months or more, the money and policy are protected because she is only prohibited from receiving Medicaid if she transfers the assets within 30 months of entering the nursing home.

Drawback

Coretta may die while holding her sister's money and life insurance policy. This can be handled by having her make a will setting up a trust for her sister's benefit. Of course, Coretta would have to choose a person to handle the trust (a trustee) and a person(s) who would get the money upon Ethel's death.

Option 2   Holding assets in trust

There are different kinds of trusts to consider here. For a complete explanation, before continuing go back and read pages 50-54.

Example: An irrevocable trust that *doesn't* protect assets

Ethel sets up The Ethel Johnson Trust naming her sister as trustee and herself as beneficiary. She gives the trustee the power to give her all, some or none of the principal and income. Since she gave discretion over the assets and income to the trustee, Medicaid assumes that the trustee will use her power and make the assets and income available to her sister. In other words, the assets are considered countable and therefore available (see page 46).

Example: **An irrevocable trust that *does* protect assets:**

Ethel sets up The Ethel Johnson Trust with the same trustee and beneficiary. This time, however, she doesn't give any power to the trustee to give her the assets, only the power to hold them in trust while they generate income for her. The day Ethel goes into the nursing home is the day the snapshot is taken of her assets. However, this time the assets in the trust are not available because the trustee has no authority to give them to her sister.

Here's what Ethel could do:

Plan A   Establish an irrevocable trust like the second example above; OR

Plan B   Establish a revocable trust naming herself as beneficiary but specifying that the trust becomes irrevocable if she goes into a nursing home or has a long-term illness.

Which plan is best?

Plan A means that Ethel gives up full control of the assets well before she goes into the home. This is the same as giving assets away.

Plan B means that Ethel's assets are countable for 30 months because revocable trusts don't protect countable assets. The trust in Plan B only becomes irrevocable when there's a long-term illness or nursing home confinement. Therefore 30 months must expire before the assets are protected. This option is useful only for people with a great deal of money who can easily afford to pay privately for 30 months. Ethel can't.

If any trust is to be used, Plan A is the best choice because Ethel has a close and trusting relationship with her sister.

Option 3   Holding assets in joint accounts

As we see in our chart, Ethel and Coretta hold their assets jointly in an "or" account. Most joint accounts are held in such a way that either co-holder can get access to the money. This is the case here. Either Ethel *or* Coretta can gain access to the account without the other's signature. Medicaid considers this type of account completely owned by

Ethel unless she can prove otherwise. Why? Because the presumption in most states is that jointly held funds belong entirely to the person going into the nursing home (see page 123).

There's another type of account that Ethel could open that requires both signatures. This is called an "and" account because both her *and* her sister's signature are required for either one to get the money.

In most states, an "and" account is protected from being spent on a nursing home if the co-holder refuses to co-sign the check or withdrawal slip to give the ill person access to the account. It remains inaccessible until the person in the nursing home dies.

In our example, if any of Ethel's investments require two signatures, Coretta could make the entire amount inaccessible by simply refusing to co-sign the withdrawal slip. Because regulations vary from state to state, be sure to check with your local welfare office to be sure an "and" account is considered inaccessible in your locale.

Drawbacks

1) As stated above, if either Ethel or Coretta can get access to the funds, Medicaid will consider them entirely owned by Ethel and they will be considered a countable asset.

2) Money held in an "and" account becomes vulnerable in two situations: First, the money becomes a countable asset to Ethel if Coretta dies before her sister. Second, even though Coretta will probably outlive her sister, their money is frozen until her sister dies.

Which of our options is best?

1) Giving away assets

2) Holding assets in trusts

3) Holding assets jointly

Option 1, giving away assets, is the best approach since the sisters have a close relationship and there are no other family members to consider.

Here is how the transferred assets line up:

non-countable	countable	inaccessible
2-family house	none	all cash held by Coretta insurance policy owned by Coretta on her sister's life

Nieces/nephews and aunts/uncles

Protecting assets for these individuals can be accomplished using the same methods discussed in examples 3 (Offspring and single parent, see page 94) and 4 (Siblings, see page 102).

Grandparents and grandchildren

Protecting assets for these individuals can be accomplished using the same methods discussed in examples 3 (Offspring and a single parent, see page 94) and 4 (Siblings, see page 102).

Unrelated people

Protecting assets for unrelated individuals can be accomplished using the same methods discussed in example 4 (Siblings, see page 102).

CHAPTER 5

WHAT TO DO WHEN YOU DON'T HAVE TIME TO PROTECT YOUR ASSETS

WHAT TO DO WHEN YOU DON'T
HAVE TIME TO PROTECT YOUR ASSETS

**There IS something
you can do!**

The whole concept of planning hinges on the disqualification period. Protecting assets even if you don't have time to plan can be accomplished if you grasp the following statement:

If someone makes a transfer of countable assets for less than fair market value within 30 months of applying for Medicaid it is presumed that the transfer was made to have Medicaid pay the nursing home bills. Therefore, the person will be disqualified from receiving Medicaid.

**Understanding the
Disqualification Rule**

The following segments interpret this all-important rule and show you how to use it to your advantage.

"If a person makes a transfer of countable assets for less than fair market value..."

Medicaid disqualifies the person going into a medical institution or nursing home for transferring only countable, *not* non-countable assets (see page 46), within 30 months. With the exception of the house, non-countable assets may be transferred to anyone, at any time, even while applying for financial assistance. In other words, you cannot be disqualified from receiving Medicaid because you transfer non-countable assets.

Protecting countable assets

Understanding non-countable assets can give you a tool to protect some assets when your back is against the wall and you don't have 30 months to plan.

At first glance, this might not be apparent because the list of exempt assets is so limited. The only non-countable assets a person can keep are the following:

- A house used as a primary residence (in most states this includes two-and three-family homes)
- An amount of cash, usually $2,000
- A car
- Personal jewelry
- Household effects
- A pre-paid funeral
- A burial account (if allowed by your state)
- Term life (as opposed to whole life) insurance policies which have no cash surrender value

For more information on what your state considers to be non-countable assets see chart 8 page 250.

With the exception of the house (see Chapter 7), most non-countable assets don't represent a lot of money. Their real value is that they can be purchased with countable assets (funds from a savings account, for instance) at any time, even while applying for Medicaid. Medicaid allows you to spend countable assets on specified goods as long as they are for fair market value and non-countable. Fair market value is defined as the going rate for goods or services. A good example of this: you could buy a reasonably-priced car for the stay-at-home spouse.

Medicaid prohibits the transfer of countable assets for other than fair market value. You can't take assets that would have to be spent on a medical institution or nursing home and get rid of them without receiving something of roughly equal value.

The same concept applies to the purchase of services. Household repairs such as replacing a leaking roof or fixing a noisy muffler in your car and various other necessary household expenses can be paid for out of a "countable" savings account, as long as the cost is consistent with the going rate.

That means that your son can't fix your muffler and charge you $2,000 without Medicaid smelling a rat.

A caution: Don't get too creative with this concept or you could get into a real pickle. There couldn't be a clearer example than a case recently decided in Massachusetts . A lawyer instructed his client to spend a great deal of cash on personal jewelry just as the person was going into a nursing home, believing that this was a way of protecting assets. When Medicaid balked, the case went to court. In arguing his case, the attorney quoted chapter and verse of the state regulation. The court didn't buy it. It held that the regulation exempting jewelry pertained to jewelry already owned by a Medicaid applicant. In any case, the legislature never intended that this type of transaction be allowed. As an aside, there's another problem with jewelry: the mark-up on new jewelry is so high that you'd be lucky to get back 25% of its original price when you sell it.

The key idea here is to be reasonable. Medicaid officials just won't be impressed by purchases of expensive items like jewelry or oriental rugs. No state will accept such items as legitimate, non-countable household items.

Example: Miguel, single, has $25,000 in a money market account and is going into a nursing home in the near future. If he transfers the money outright to his relatives, he will be disqualified from receiving Medicaid for 30 months.

In most states Miguel would be allowed to purchase a pre-paid funeral, open a burial account (up to a specified amount), purchase household goods, and even pay outstanding or necessary bills like utilities, rent, or mortgage and personal bills such as credit cards.

This means that Miguel's funeral and other expenses will be paid out of his money, not his family's.

Example: Edward and Mary have $50,000 in savings. They didn't have time to plan before Mary went into a nursing home on May 1. Under the law in most states, Edward can only keep one half of the assets. However, Mary is allowed to buy with her $25,000 a number of non-countable assets, as Miguel could in our example above.

Let's take this example one step farther. In addition to

the assets, Edward and Mary have a house with a $10,000 mortgage remaining on it and a car loan. In most states, the law allows Mary to pay off the entire mortgage and car loan from her funds only.

The benefits are obvious. Mary can convert non-exempt assets to exempt assets. She can use funds which otherwise would go to the nursing home to pay off major debts and some lesser expenses such as a pre-paid funeral and some household items and repairs.

"...within 30 months of applying for Medicaid..."

Medicaid is suspicious of any transfer of countable assets within 30 months of requesting Medicaid. You now understand that countable assets must be transferred at least 30 months before . But what happens if someone is already institutionalized? Does the 30-month rule still apply? Yes! You will have to pay privately for 30 months after moving the assets, but after that the countable assets are protected. Remember: Never apply for Medicaid until the 30-month qualification period has expired (see pages 65-66).

Example: Andrew, single, has $200,000 in cash. He goes into a nursing home on January 1, 1991. He is allowed to transfer all his funds to anyone even after he has been admitted. Yes, he IS disqualified for 30 months from receiving Medicaid and must pay privately. But that's his maximum exposure—30 months. If it costs $30,000 a year, Andrew will have spent $75,000. He has saved $125,000.

Remember: If you or your spouse went into a nursing home prior to October, 1989, never apply for Medicaid until the 30-month disqualification period has expired. There are still many states that apply their own laws which say that applying for Medicaid within that 30-month period would disqualify you until *all* the transferred assets are spent, not just until the end of the 30-month period.

Example: Maureen went into a nursing home in July of 1989. She transferred $60,000 to her daughter at that time and she kept $60,000 to pay for about 30 months of nursing home care (this protects the money that was transferred). However, she accidentally applies for Medicaid 28 months after the transfer. The state could disqualify her not just for the *remaining two months but until all the transferred money is used up paying the nursing home bills.*

"...it is presumed that the transfer was made to have Medicaid pay the nursing home bills."

Medicaid presumes that the transfer of countable assets for less than fair market value within 30 months of applying for Medicaid was made to hide those assets. Any presumption can be rebutted. In most states (make sure you check with your Department of Public Welfare), if you can show that at the time the transfer was made there was a legitimate reason for the transfer, those assets are protected and do not have to be spent as countable assets.

Here is a list of what most states consider to be legitimate transfers:

1) At the time countable assets were given away, you were in good health with no medical history of the illness(es) that put you in a nursing home.

2) You had established a pattern of making transfers or gifts, such as reducing the size of your estate for tax purposes, or helping your grandchildren pay for college.

3) At the time you made the transfer or gift, you retained enough countable assets to pay for your then-anticipated medical expenses.

4) At the time you made the transfer or gifts, you were not, nor was your family, aware of the Medicaid regulations on transfer of assets.

Example: Roger, a divorced father of two college-age children, has a savings account of $50,000. For the past three years, he has contributed $2,000 to each child for college expenses. He has no record of major health problems.

Roger suffers a stroke which necessitates nursing home care. He is allowed to take the balance of his savings account ($44,000) and buy non-countable assets (see page 46). Moreover, if his offspring can prove any one or all of the above criteria, they may not have to give the tuition money back to their father to be spent as a countable asset and Roger will qualify for financial assistance.

These criteria apply to anyone, single or married, who makes a gift or transfers countable assets within 30 months of going into a nursing home. The disqualification period may be less based upon the amount, transferred (see page 131).

A note about gift taxes

Federal gift tax applies only if the person giving away assets has more than $600,000. In other words, you *can* give away more than $10,000 a year without paying a federal gift tax. Most states do not have a gift tax but be sure to check with your state Department of Revenue.

How are you holding your assets? The "AND" word

Most people hold their assets with someone else. These "or" accounts are set up in such a way that either one *or* the other co-holder can get the money without the permission of the other. However, there are certain types of investments that require two or more signatures to get access. These are called "and" accounts.

Under the law in most states (make sure you check with your Department of Welfare), all "or" accounts held by husband or wife are joint assets subject to division. Worse still, if you hold your investments with anyone other than your husband or wife, they are presumed to be 100 percent the property of the person going into the medical institution or nursing home.

"And" accounts are given special protection. In some states (make sure you check with your Department of Welfare) the account becomes inaccessible or unavailable (see page 49) to the person going into the nursing home if the co-holder refuses to give permission (in the form of a signature) to get access to the funds. They remain inaccessible until the death of either co-holder. Parents generally set up these accounts with their offspring.

There are two drawbacks to "and" accounts:

First, if the co-holder dies before the person in the nursing home, the money becomes a countable asset to the patient. He will then be disqualified from receiving assistance until it is spent down.

Second, the money is frozen until the person in the nursing home dies since the co-holder can't get access without the patient's signature. Money taken at any time could well be considered the patient's and therefore a countable asset.

Special cases

If you are holding your assets jointly with someone, there are a number of ways your account might be set up. The following is a list of commonly used titles on investments:

1) A in trust for B
2) A payable on death (POD) to B
3) A or B as tenants in common
4) A and B as joint tenants with right of survivorship (JTWROS)

In numbers 1 and 2, A (typically a parent, grandparent or sibling) owns 100% of the account, not B. If B goes into the nursing home, the money is not considered his.

In number 3, the money usually belongs to the person who goes into the nursing home first, regardless of whose name is first.

Number 4 is considered an "and" account.

There are serious dangers in holding assets with a friend or a sibling. If he is institutionalized before you, Medicaid will presume that the assets belong entirely to him. The key word here is *presume*. In a crisis, most states (make sure to check with your Department of Public Welfare) allow the co-holder to show that he either owns the assets or made a contribution to them in some proportion.

Evidence that can be presented includes a social security number on an account and records of deposits and withdrawals. Also helpful would be to show that the Medicaid applicant's signature was only on the account for convenience, as indicated through documents such as letters. In other words, if it's your money but the co-holder is institutionalized, you would be allowed to keep the money if you could show through evidence that in fact some or all of the money is yours.

You are well advised to look closely at how you are holding accounts, especially if you are single or widowed. Single parents tend to hold their money either with their children or siblings. If money is held with your children, it is considered 100% yours. If with your sibling, the money is considered 100% owned by the person who goes in first unless you can prove it's yours.

This can cause difficulties. For example, if these funds were in a CD that had been rolled over for years, there's no way of proving what funds are yours since there are no deposits or withdrawals.

Two important things to remember:

1) As with other asset transfers, these accounts must be set up at least two and a half years prior to applying for Medicaid.

2) The law is unresolved as to whether holding assets in an "and" account between a husband and wife will offer protection since the stay-at-home spouse is part of the application process.

Spousal transfers within the Disqualification Period

Medicaid gives a certain degree of protection to assets held by husbands and wives. The Spousal Impoverishment Act (SIA) considers all countable assets, regardless of whose name they are in, to be jointly held and available for division on the day the spouse goes into a medical institution or nursing home. For a further explanation see page 55.

Medicaid allows unlimited transfers of countable assets between husband and wife at any time even if the transfer takes place within 30 months of a spouse's institutionalization. However, if the spouse who receives the assets transfers them to a third party, such as a child, within 30 months, the ill spouse will be disqualified for Medicaid benefits.

Example: Gunther and his wife Anna have total countable assets of $50,000. Of this, $40,000 is held in Gunther's IRA account which is in his name only. Gunther is allowed to transfer his IRA to his wife even within 30 months of his going into a nursing home. Anna, however, cannot turn around and give that money to her children without causing Gunther to lose Medicaid benefits.

Medicaid's goal in prohibiting Anna from transferring assets is to have them available for division the day her husband is institutionalized.

Spousal Refusal

There is an alternative to having one half or more of these assets spent on Gunther's care. Let's say that Anna, who now has all the money in her name only, refuses to give one half to the nursing home for her husband's care. This is called **Spousal Refusal.**

There's a technicality that applies in a case like this

that has to do with spouses' rights in divorce situations. Although no divorce is contemplated here, Gunther and Anna each would have certain rights to marital assets in the event of a divorce.

All states divide marital assets based on a number of factors. By law, Gunther can give his rights to marital assets to Medicaid. This is called an assignment of rights. If he does, Medicaid must qualify him for benefits immediately.

Medicaid now has the right to sue Anna for marital assets. Remember, we're not suggesting that Anna file for divorce. Nor are we suggesting that Medicaid will make her divorce her husband. Medicaid simply has the right to go to court to collect whatever assets Gunther might have been entitled to in the hypothetical event of a divorce.

So what's the purpose of this legal maneuver?

Most states have special courts that deal with divorce. Medicaid can only sue in those courts. It is likely that the court would give Anna a more generous division of assets than Medicaid regulations would allow. In considering this option, you must weigh the expense of attorneys' fees against the additional monies you might receive from the court beyond what Medicaid already allows.

Note: If Gunther is totally incapacitated, Medicaid will pay for him if his doctor writes a report stating that he is too ill to perform the necessary actions to get to his assets.

Example: Gunther and Anna have countable assets of $150,000. Under the Spousal Impoverishment Act she is allowed to keep only up to $66,480. Most states will usually divide assets equally in a divorce. There is an excellent chance Anna would be allowed to keep at least $75,000 if Medicaid sued her in probate court.

Appealing Medicaid decisions on asset division

This option is available only to spouses. As we discussed earlier, a non-institutionalized spouse is allowed to keep an amount of money when the husband or wife goes into a chronic care facility or nursing home. This can range from a low of $13,296 to a maximum of $66,480 depending upon state regulations (see chart 1 page 241). The Spousal Impoverishment Act does allow for an appeal process. Each state has an appeal system for spouses who feel that the money they have left after asset division will not generate enough income to live on. If you believe that the assets left to the stay-at-home spouse are not sufficient to generate income, you can ask for an appeals hearing through your local Department of Public Welfare.

Preserving "half-a-loaf"

As we've seen, the federal government has set 30 months as the maximum period during which a person who has transferred assets can be disqualified from receiving Medicaid benefits (see page 64).

However, here's something we haven't looked at yet because it's not relevant when you're planning ahead. We need to look at it now because it can be a lifesaver when you're out of time and your back is against the wall. It's called the "half-a-loaf" rule.

In some cases, under this rule the disqualification period may be shorter. For example, the disqualification ends when all the money that was transferred has been spent for a person's care. That makes sense. Now here's the lifesaver, the "half-a-loaf" rule: Federal law states you are disqualified for 30 months **OR** for a period of time that is determined by taking the amount of money transferred and dividing it by the average monthly nursing home bill in your area, as determined by your Department of Public Welfare.

For instance, let's say the average nursing home cost as determined by your state is $3,000 a month. If you transfer $30,000 the day you go into a nursing home, you will be disqualified for 10 months, the number of months that result from taking $30,000 and dividing it by $3,000. What if you have $60,000? Could you take $30,000 of it and protect it by giving it away? Yes, because you are not disqualified for 30 months, but rather only ten months. The remaining $30,000 would be used to pay for all or most of the ten months you're disqualified. In effect, by transferring your assets you've protected half the loaf.

Example: Bill, a widower, has $90,000 in cash. He goes into a nursing home on January 1, 1991. He transfers $45,000 on that date. Let's say his state sets the average monthly nursing home cost at $3,000. Therefore, he is disqualified for 15 months ($45,000 divided by $3,000). During that period he pays with the $45,000 that wasn't transferred. If the

*actual nursing home cost is $3,000, he has protected
the entire amount he transferred. On the other hand,
if the actual nursing home cost is $3,500 a month, he
would have to pay the difference ($7,500) out of his
transferred monies — $500 a month times the
number of months (15) he is disqualified.*

If all of his money were transferred, he would still
not face a maximum 30 month disqualification, but
rather will qualify for Medicaid when the money is
actually spent on his care.

What if he transfers none of his assets? He has to
spend down to whatever he is allowed to keep in
non-countable assets (see page 46). He loses almost
everything.

*Example: Vincent and Dottie have $120,000 in
countable assets. Dottie is in a nursing home. The
state they live in allows the stay-at-home spouse to
keep one half the assets (up to the federal limit of
$66,480). Under this rule, Vincent would be allowed to
keep $60,000, and Dottie would have to spend
$60,000. Their state has set the average monthly
nursing home cost at $3,000.*

Dottie can transfer one half of her half of the assets

($30,000) to an offspring. As in the previous example, Dottie will now be disqualified for ten months. If her monthly nursing home bill actually is $3,000, the bills during that disqualification period will be paid for entirely by the money remaining in Dottie's name. Any costs over that amount would have to be absorbed by the person to whom the assets were transferred or by Dottie's social security or other income.

To see if the half-a-loaf rule helps you, call your Department of Public Welfare to find out the average monthly nursing home cost as determined by your state. Divide that amount into the amount of assets you possess. That figure determines how much money you have at risk (your "exposure").

Note: The above technique works only if the average monthly nursing home cost established by your Department of Public Welfare closely matches your actual monthly bill. If the actual bill is, say, $1,000 or more higher, a quick calculation will show you that you will have to substantially invade the money you transferred in order to cover expenses during the months you are disqualified.

Insult to injury – Suing your spouse for divorce

Under the Spousal Impoverishment Act (SIA), the maximum a stay-at-home spouse is allowed to keep from joint assets is $66,480. Couples with more than $133,960 in assets may want to consider the possibility of divorce proceedings.

This option, like the above, applies only to spouses. SIA provides that a court may make a division of assets that may be more favorable than Medicaid allows.

Example: Evan and Lillian have joint countable assets of $150,000 on the day Lillian goes into a nursing home. Under SIA, all Evan could keep is one half of the total assets or $66,480, whichever is less. However, if Evan were to file a divorce petition, it is likely he would get at least half ($75,000) of their joint property and maybe more, depending upon his financial circumstances.

Example: George is married with two children. While watching television one day, he collapses. He is rushed to the hospital and diagnosed as having had a severe stroke. His prognosis: He will be in a coma for the rest *of his life. George is 46 years old. The family's total assets — an $80,000 IRA.*

Under Medicaid regulations, all George's wife could keep of countable assets is one half of her husband's IRA ($40,000). By filing an action for divorce she could request from the court more than half based on her limited earning capacity and the needs of two minor children.

Filing for divorce usually should not be considered unless you have first filed and lost an appeal to the Department of Public Welfare. This is a complicated procedure that should only be done with the assistance of a lawyer.

Protecting assets by claiming disability

In Chapter 3, we discussed a group of assets which Medicaid could not reach because the person going into the nursing home couldn't reach them. These are called inaccessible assets. In most states (make sure you check with your Department of Public Welfare), monies can be protected if you can show that the person applying for Medicaid cannot get access to them because he or she is too sick. The investments remain frozen until the person dies.

Example: *Eduardo, who is single, is on life support systems. He has $50,000 in his name alone which would be countable and therefore spent on a nursing home. If someone can present evidence to Medicaid that Eduardo cannot gain access because of his condition, the money remains intact and he would qualify for Medicaid immediately. Medicaid may require that a guardian or conservator be appointed (see pages 197-198) to gain access to Eduardo's accounts. Even if Medicaid did not force the issue they could put a lien on the estate after he died. The practical effect of claiming disability is that although Medicaid will get reimbursed from the estate, it will be at a much lower rate than the private pay rate, so there may be something left for the heirs.*

Catastrophic consequences

What happens if you transfer your assets to someone you trust, and through misfortune or irresponsibility the assets are lost? Every state has in its regulations a provision suspending the disqualification period if you can show that enforcing the rule would have catastrophic results.

Example: Susan transfers $35,000 to her daughter who promptly spends it. Susan is now asking Medicaid to pay for her nursing home care. She tells them that she has transferred the funds within 30 months of her request for assistance. She still may receive Medicaid if she or her doctor can show that a discharge from the nursing home or failure to be admitted could cause her death or serious further health problems.

Don't let the nursing home or the Medicaid office dictate terms in circumstances like these. Go directly to the Medicaid appeals process to argue in favor of eligibility because of an emergency situation. Also contact your office of elder affairs to find out what steps can be taken to keep the nursing home from discharging your relative.

PROTECTING INCOME FROM MEDICAID

Most of an unmarried person's income cannot be protected from a nursing home or other long-term care institution. There are two exceptions: He may keep 1) a small personal needs account, and 2) premiums for health care coverage such as Medigap. However, Medicaid makes a provision for married couples that allows the stay-at-home spouse to keep a portion of combined income.

Spousal Impoverishment Act guidelines

Under the Spousal Impoverishment Act, a non-institutionalized spouse may be allowed to keep a certain amount of his or her spouse's earned income. Income is defined as any money received from investments, pensions, social security, trusts, royalties, etc. received by either party. The minimum amount the states allow the stay-at-home spouse to keep is $856 per month; the maximum is $1,662 monthly plus certain additional allowances (these amounts will increase automatically each year). The stay-at-home spouse may be entitled to additional monies if she can show that housing and utility expenses exceed 30% of the monthly amount the state allows her to keep.

Example: *Louis and Mae are married with a total*

income of $2,200 a month, broken down as follows:

Louis has $800 in social security and a pension of $1,200.

Mae has $200 in social security.

If their state allowed Mae to keep only the minimum of $856, she would be able to keep $656 of her husband's income in addition to her $200. The rest would go to the nursing home with the exception of a small personal needs account for him and a deduction for his Medigap payment.

If their state allowed Mae to keep $1,300 a month she would then be allowed to keep $1,100 of his income in addition to her $200.

Note: The state allows a stay-at-home spouse to keep all her income including that earned from working and income from the assets she is allowed to keep. If Mae has monthly income from a part-time job of $1500, she does not have to give money to her husband; she just would not be able to get any of his income. Our example uses a wife as a stay-at-home spouse, but the rules apply just the same if the husband is at home.

Shelter Allowance

The stay-at-home spouse may be entitled to additional monies (a shelter allowance) if she can show that the monthly maintenance allowance ($856) is insufficient to keep up her house. There is a formula that Medicaid uses to figure out the maximum additional allowance. The figuring is complicated and best explained by an example.

Walter is in a nursing home and has qualified for Medicaid. His monthly income is $1,200. His wife Nora continues to live at home. Her income is $450 from social security. The mortgage on the house is $700 per month and the utilities are $200 monthly.

Here are the steps that Nora should take to determine if she can get more than $856 a month.

1. Add the monthly amount that Nora pays for her mortgage ($700) and utilities ($200), for a total of $900.

2. Take 30% of $856, Nora's standard monthly maintenance allowance. That amount is $256.80.

3. Deduct $256.80 from the total amount Nora pays for her mortgage and utilities ($900.) $900 minus

$256.80 equals $643.20, called her excess shelter allowance.

4. Add $856 and $643.2 = $1,499.20.

5. Deduct Nora's monthly income ($450) from $1,499.20

6. The figure arrived at in step 5 is Nora's new monthly maintenance allowance.

$856.00	Nora's standard monthly maintenance allowance
+ 643.20 =1499.20	excess shelter allowance, see 2 and 3 above
− 450.00	Nora's monthly income from social security
$1,049.20	Nora's new monthly maintenance allowance

The question the stay-at-home spouse must ask is: Does she think that her monthly housing expenses eat up too much of her monthly maintenance allowance? Always assume that they do and use the above formula to see if you may be entitled to more than the minimum.

Remember: The only unquestioned increase that Medicaid allows in the monthly maintenance amount is to cover mortgage, rent and utilities.

Other ways to secure more income

Spouses who cannot survive financially on the allowance given to them by Medicaid can appeal directly to the state's welfare office. You must show that the income available is not sufficient to cover your needs because of extraordinary expenses or unusual circumstances. Be prepared to document your request.

Basically, what the spouse is asking for is alimony that federal law allows to be deducted from the institutionalized spouse's income.

Example: Peter is in a nursing home. His monthly income from his pension is $2,700. His wife Cheryl has $300 from social security. The state they live in only allows Cheryl to keep a maximum of $1,662 a month. Let's assume that even with an excess shelter allowance she would still not have enough money for *her monthly expenses. She could petition the state for more of her husband's income but it is doubtful they would grant her request.*

Finally, SIA does allow the stay-at-home spouse to file either a divorce or a separate maintenance petition in the family or probate court that handles domestic relations to secure more income than Medicaid would allow.

A note about **"cap states"** (chart 3, page 243): These are states that deny Medicaid eligibility to individuals whose net monthly income exceeds a certain amount even though it does not cover his nursing home bill. Rules are usually different for married couples. If you live in a cap state and you are anticipating a nursing home placement, it is crucial that you seek legal assistance to determine if income can be shifted.

CHAPTER 7

PROTECTING THE HOUSE –
A VERY SPECIAL ASSET

Understanding the law

Every state has the power to place a lien on a person's home to recover the cost of nursing home care. Generally, the lien can only be placed on a home after the Medicaid recipient's death, assuming there is no surviving spouse. Currently, a surviving spouse can remain in the house without a lien, making it possible for her to transfer the property to her children or anyone else.

The federal government gave the states the option of taking your house sooner rather than waiting until you die. A state can reclassify your house as a non-exempt asset if you are single, in a nursing home and cannot show that you'll be coming home within six months (see chart 7, page 247). The state can then insist that the house be sold to pay your nursing home bills; or if you refuse, your Medicaid benefits could be terminated.

Suppose your house is sold and the money is used to pay your nursing home bills; what happens if you recover and leave the nursing home? Good question. Bad news. You're homeless.

Prior to July 1, 1988, states had different interpretations of Medicaid regulations. Since Medicaid is funded half by the states and half by the federal government, each state felt free to adopt rules that suited its particular circumstances. As a result, there was little uniformity.

Although the states agree on little, everyone seems to support the notion that a person's home is a very special asset that should be given certain protections that ordinary assets don't have. Most states allow the primary residence to remain a non-countable asset even if no one lives there. Many states used to allow the house to be transferred to family members or anyone else, not only within 30 months of requesting Medicaid, but even if the person making the transfer is on Medicaid!

But wait for a moment. Is it fair to allow a Medicaid recipient to transfer the house solely for the purpose of avoiding repayment of money paid on their behalf? Put another way, should the taxpayer be subsidizing inheritances? Most of us would answer a resounding "No"— with one exception: If the house being transferred belongs to a member of *our* family or a friend.

Congress realized that the states did not have the political backbone to prohibit these transfers. If any state representative voted to place a lien on a voter's property he wouldn't have a prayer of getting re-elected.

As of July 1, 1988, Congress mandated that the states adopt, within approximately a year and a half, the following rules regarding the transfer of a house:

For single persons: A transfer of the house to anyone within 30 months of applying for Medicaid triggers a disqualification from Medicaid until either 30 months passes or the nursing home bills accumulate to the value of the house.

Example: Lee has a house worth $65,000. She transfers it to her sister for $1.00 in January, 1990. She will be disqualified from receiving Medicaid until July, 1992 (30 months) or until the value of her nursing home bills exceeds $65,000. Let's say that Lee goes into a nursing home six months later and that the cost is $42,000 a year. Lee will continue to be disqualified for two more years unless she spends the value of her house ($65,000) on her nursing home bills. Since $65,000 pays for approximately 19 months, she will qualify for Medicaid before 30 months, in February, 1992.

For couples: Either spouse is allowed to transfer, without penalty, his or her interest in their home to the other spouse at any time, even while on

Medicaid. The spouse who becomes sole owner of the home could transfer it to another party.

When the institutionalized spouse dies, the surviving spouse is free to transfer the property without penalty. In other words, even though Medicaid paid, the house cannot be used for reimbursement.

Example: Jerry and Bess are married and own a house jointly. Bess goes into a nursing home on June 1,1991. She is allowed to sign over her interest to her husband even though she may request Medicaid within 30 months. Jerry could transfer the property without disqualifying his wife while his wife is alive.

1) If Bess dies having been on Medicaid, and Jerry dies with the property in his name, Medicaid may put a lien on it.

2) If Jerry dies before Bess, and doesn't change his will (in which like most husbands, he leaves everything to the wife), the property immediately goes to her and is subject to a lien at her death.

Exceptions to prohibition against transferring

When you transfer your house, Medicaid disqualifies you for eligibility for benefits except in certain cases. A single person or married couple can transfer a home to:

1) a child who is blind, disabled or under 21.

2) a sibling who owns a share of the home and has resided there for at least one year before the co-holder goes into the nursing home.

3) a child (of any age) who has resided in the home for at least two years before the parent's institutional-ization and can show that he has cared for the parent at home.

4) anyone at any time as long as it is for fair market value.

5) anyone, providing the purpose of the transfer is not to qualify for Medicaid. For example, a person gives his house to his children while healthy for the purpose of avoiding probate or estate taxes. Later, he is permanently disabled in an accident and is forced to go into a nursing home within 30 months of making the transfer.

This transfer would probably not disqualify him for Medicaid.

One last possibility — Even though the transfer of a house would ordinarily disqualify a person for Medicaid, he may still receive benefits if he can show that he would suffer undue hardship by not being granted benefits. This alternative is rarely accepted by Medicaid.

Who can and who can't transfer a home

There are four options for protecting your home if you have 30 months or more to plan. They are:

Give away the house
Give away the house with a life estate
Put the house in trust
Hold the house jointly

Give away the house

A person is free to give a house to whomever he chooses and later qualify for Medicaid providing the transfer takes place at least 30 months prior to institutionalization or application for Medicaid. There are three considerations before you do this.

First, giving your home away leaves you with no control. There are more than a few cases of a daughter who has tried to have parents evicted from their home or a son who has lost the house through bad investments or a divorce.

Second, while you may trust the person or persons to whom you give your house, you sacrifice the one-time $125,000 exemption from capital gains taxes (assuming you are over 55) if you later decide to sell (see page 224).

Third, by giving away your home, you pass on to the receiver a greater capital gains tax liability when the house is sold. Capital gains is the difference between the basis (what you paid for the house plus what you spent on major improvements) and the sale price. Most older Americans paid relatively little for their homes and have seen their homes appreciate greatly in value. This low basis is passed on to the recipient of the house. When she later sells the property at fair market value, she pays a substantial tax on the capital gain (see pages 224-227).

Give away the house with a life estate

When a person gives away his house he may make a provision that he keep an interest in the property for the remainder of his life. That interest may take the form of a life estate through which he has a lifelong right to live in the home as well as to receive any income or benefits that may accrue from the property.

A life estate does not mean that you *own* the property; it means that you have an *interest* that ends when you die. Medicaid can only place a lien on your property to recoup nursing home expenses if you alone legally own the property when you die. A life estate is a very good way to protect your house from a Medicaid lien (see page 229).

In addition, there are significant tax advantages. You may be able to claim a portion or all of the capital gains exemption if the property is sold during your life. The recipient also avoids the problems we discuss above when the house is eventually sold. See your accountant for a complete explanation of the tax savings (see chapter 14).

Put the house in trust

For an explanation of different kinds of trusts, please read pages 50-54. In that chapter, we see that revocable trusts can't be used to protect *countable* assets. But remember, your house is a *non-countable* asset (see page 46). Therefore, placing it in a revocable trust (even though it's an instrument you fully control) does not, in most states, jeopardize Medicaid eligibility.

In most states, liens are not placed on the Medicaid recipient's home until he dies and then only if the property is in his name only. A home placed in a revocable trust is owned by the trust, not the Medicaid recipient. It stands to reason that if there's nothing in the recipient's name, no lien can be attached. (Be sure to check with an attorney to see how your state treats revocable trusts.)

The advantages of a revocable trust are that it:

1) gives the homeowner (called the "grantor") absolute control over the property during his lifetime including the right to be the trustee, if he chooses.

2) does away with the need for a co-owner of the property.

3) gives the person who set up the trust (if over age 55) the entire $125,000 capital gains exemption if the property is sold during his life.

4) avoids probate.

5) minimizes capital gains.

Note: In some states legislators are considering placing liens on homes when the applicant first goes into a nursing home. Therefore, although the house can be transferred, the lien goes with it. When the house is sold, Medicaid would get reimbursed. Be sure to check with your Department of Public Welfare to find out what regulations apply in your state.

Holding the house jointly

A single or widowed person may consider holding his house jointly with the person who will eventually inherit it. However, joint ownership is both impractical and dangerous. Impractical, because you no longer have full control over the property. Dangerous, because the co-holder may go into a nursing home before you do.

For example, if Medicaid does not consider the house the primary residence of the institutionalized co-holder, it would have to be sold and one half the proceeds spent on his nursing home bills.

Other problems: You may decide to sell the house. Co-holding costs you at least one half of the capital gains exemption (assuming you are over 55).

What if your co-holder gets a divorce and the house is considered part of the couple's common property? Or your co-holder may get sued.

If you must hold property jointly, make sure you do so with a younger person such as your son or daughter, and insist that he or she enter into an agreement with the spouse that exempts the property from their joint marital assets.

Does holding the house jointly avoid a lien?

Since Medicaid liens are only placed on a single person's home, in most states, certain kinds of joint ownership avoids a Medicaid lien. The two most common forms of co-ownership are joint tenancy (Steve Smith *and* Carl Jones) and tenants in common (Steve Smith *or* Carl Jones).

Joint tenancy means that if Steve dies, Carl automatically gets his share of the property and vice versa.

Tenants in common means that if Steve dies, his heirs get his share automatically, not Carl; and if Carl dies, his heirs automatically get his share of the property, not Steve.

Property held in joint tenancy in most states is protected from a lien because the share belonging to the deceased co-owner never goes through his estate. Instead, it goes automatically to the surviving co-holder. Not so with tenants in common. The share belonging to the deceased co-holder goes through his estate, which immediately makes it available for a lien.

If you are single, as a way of avoiding a Medicaid lien, you may choose to hold your home in a joint tenancy with someone else.

Warning: States have varying regulations covering this issue. Your state may not agree with the above interpretation. They may hold that a lien attaches to the deceased's one half share even though it doesn't go through probate. Be sure to check with an attorney or your local welfare office.

Panic – There's no time to plan

No time to plan means that a person will be going into a medical institution or nursing home or requesting Medicaid assistance within 30 months of transferring his home. Obviously, if you are facing this situation, your first concern is to protect your house.

Married couple There's no problem here since the law allows the person going into the nursing home to transfer his interest to the spouse even while on Medicaid. Under present regulations, the spouse who now has the house in her name can give it away or sell it while her husband is alive or after his death without penalty.

Single people Transferring your house within 30 months of going into a nursing home poses a difficult situation for single people. Your best option is to see if you fall into any of the exceptions mentioned on page 152. If you don't, here's a grim option:

Don't try to transfer the house at all if it is worth a great deal of money (say, over $200,000). Medicaid *will* place a lien on it when you die. But since Medicaid usually pays about two-thirds of the private daily rate, the bite out of your estate will be less than if you pay privately for institutionalization.

For example, if a nursing home charges private pay patients $100 a day, the rate that Medicaid pays for the same person is about $75. Upon your death your family will have to pay the lien, but it's two-thirds of what the private rate would have been.

The only problem is that your state may have

adopted the federal regulation which mandates that
a primary residence be sold after six months of
institutionalization if the patient cannot show that
he will be returning home. Check with your local
Department of Public Welfare.

THE INSURANCE DILEMMA

Until recently, few people understood that Medicare and all other forms of health insurance do not pay for custodial care in a nursing home. Because of recent media exposure given to the subject of catastrophic illness, more people have begun to face the seriousness of the problem. When an illness strikes that requires long-term custodial care, there are only three alternatives to pay: cash, Medicaid and nursing home insurance.

Nursing home insurance pays a certain amount per day for a set number of months of custodial care. There is a desperate need for such policies. Unfortunately, the truth is that finding a good policy is very difficult at this time.

Medigap Policies

Insurance companies spend millions of dollars annually advertising the virtues of policies that take up where Medicare leaves off. Elderly people are frequently targeted by aggressive agents who sell them multiple policies with overlapping and therefore virtually useless coverage. Many people buy them believing that they are covered for nursing home care. With celebrity endorsements and comforting names, these policies lull older

Americans into a false sense of security.

It's an expensive mistake. None of these plans covers custodial care in nursing homes. At best, they pay some of the deductibles that Medicare doesn't cover.

Because of the industry's sorry record of abuses, there are new federal laws which mandate changes in the design and selling of Medigap policies beginning in 1992. Your state insurance commissioner or local office on aging can give you information about Medigap policies. A report on abuses in the sale of Medigap insurance and what the states are doing about them is available FREE from the Office of Public Affairs, Health Care Financing Administration, Room 435-H, 200 Independence Ave., Washington, D.C. 20201.

The most important thing to understand about insurance is this: If you want coverage for a nursing home, you have to buy a *nursing home or long-term care policy.*

Long-Term Care Insurance

Smelling profits to be made from worried seniors, the insurance industry has been designing scores of long-term care policies and hustling their agents to sell them. In the last few years, 130 insurance companies have come up some variation on the theme. An estimated 1.5 million people have bought these policies, and sales are rising by 35 percent annually.

Unfortunately, most of these products aren't worth the paper they're written on. But that doesn't mean that nursing home insurance is a bad idea. In fact, in certain cases, it may make some sense.

Assuming you find the right policy, and that's a big assumption, nursing home insurance is primarily useful for one thing — maintaining control over your assets until you need nursing home care. This book has presented a number of ways you can protect assets in the event of a long-term nursing home stay if you have time to plan. Every option, in one form or another, involves giving up control at least 30 months before going into a nursing home.

This gives rise to a dilemma: The best time to protect your life savings is when you're healthy. However, to do it you generally have to give away your assets and relinquish control. Let's say you decide it's worth it and strip away all your assets. But suppose you never need a nursing home — you die peacefully in your own bed twenty years later. For two decades, you live with the discomfort of not being in control of your finances. Not an easy decision to live with.

Here's another idea: A nursing home insurance policy can buy you time. Here's how: It allows you to maintain control of your countable assets until you need a nursing home, and, in some cases, permits you to transfer those assets with less economic consequence to you. You are covered, partially or fully, by the policy for the 30 month disqualification period during which you do not receive Medicaid.

Note: If you are considering a nursing home policy, you must plan how the assets would be taken out of your name if you were institutionalized and too incapacitated to move them yourself. The 30 month period only starts to run when assets are removed from your name. This problem can be overcome in two ways — hold your assets jointly or put together a power of attorney (see page 194).

Example: Noreen is 65 years old and widowed. She has two children. She has a house and $135,000 in cash and securities. She has two options to protect her assets from a nursing home: While she's still healthy, she can give away her assets in any number of ways. If at least 30 months go by between the date of transfer and the date of confinement, the assets are protected. However, since she's healthy, years will probably pass before she needs a nursing home — if ever.

Or she can buy a nursing home insurance policy.

Like most people, Noreen wants to keep her financial independence. She doesn't want to worry about what the answer might be if she goes to her kids and asks for her money. She doesn't want to worry about her kids getting sued or divorced and thereby jeopardizing the assets. In short, she wants control.

To keep control, she purchases a policy that pays, for example, $100 a day for custodial care in a nursing home for three years. She has a stroke in five years. She can now transfer her assets to her children or whomever she wants, even on or after the day she goes into the home.

Although the transfer disqualifies Noreen from receiving Medicaid benefits for 30 months, the policy steps in and pays the first $100 per day for that disqualification period. If Noreen did not have this *policy, she might have lost all or most of her assets and a lien might have been put on her house when she died.*

A good policy for a person in reasonably good health, at age 65, averages between $1,200 and $2,400 a year. That's expensive but the alternatives of giving away your assets or placing them in an irrevocable trust to protect them will cost you too. Give away assets and you give away control. Whether it's outright or in an irrevocable trust, you're always going to have to go to someone and ask permission to get your money.

Giving away assets can be an expensive proposition as well. Most retired people are in a lower federal tax bracket (15%) than their children (28%). If your offspring hold your assets, you pay a 13% penalty yearly. For example $100,000 generates about $8,000 a year in interest. The tax on those earnings, in a 15% bracket, is about $1,200. If your children are in a 28% bracket, the tax would almost double.

Even if you can accept the additional tax, you will find it difficult to live with this: Nursing homes avoid taking welfare patients even though it's illegal to do so. Most likely, you would have to come up with at least six to nine months of private funds to get into a first class facility near your family. That means the people who hold your money have to turn over a good chunk of it to "grease the skids" to get you in.

How much for six to nine months? In 10 years, figure in the neighborhood of $50,000 to $75,000. Nice neighborhood. Add to that the tax penalty you've paid over the years.

On the other hand, let's say that you pay $2,000 a year for a policy for 10 years. At first glance, this seems like a great deal of money. But wait. Do the arithmetic. Ten years of premiums at $2,000 per year is $20,000. That's a lot better than $50,000 to $75,000 plus taxes. And the policy usually pays for at least 36 months, assuring you of a bed in a nursing home.

The benefits are appealing. The problem is that a report issued by the Families USA Foundation found that only about 15 percent of the elderly population can afford even a minimal policy that provides only partial coverage, let alone one like the above costing $2,000 or more annually for relatively extensive coverage. And that price covers only one spouse! Of that figure, perhaps only half are young enough or healthy enough to qualify for that rate. For the vast majority of senior citizens, nursing home policies are just too expensive.

If you are one of the minority who are not staggered by the cost of premiums and you want to protect substantial assets, you may decide to look into nursing home insurance. You want to maintain control of your assets. As a responsible person, you don't want to be a burden to your family or society. You're ready to start shopping for coverage. Unfortunately, it's not that simple.

For many reasons, buying long-term care (LTC) insurance is as confusing and perilous as buying a used car. The problem is that nursing home insurance is a relatively new product and insurance companies are struggling to figure out what kinds of coverage they can make a profit on. To protect themselves, they offer policies that are worded in such a way that the insurer has a back door out of paying you the coverage you thought you were buying.

Is this deliberate deception? Maybe. On top of that, the agent may not know much about what he is selling you, or he may misrepresent the policy in order to make a sale. Like a used car, you may buy a policy that looks good but is actually a lemon and you won't find out till it's too late. When it comes time to collect, an ambiguously worded provision may disqualify you from receiving any benefits. When you buy a nursing home insurance policy you may be buying a nightmare.

If you can get past the prohibitive cost, there are many reasons why nursing home insurance may not provide you with the protection you want. One of the most important is inflation.

To understand how inflation affects this kind of insurance, let's look at Massachusetts, a state that has been a pioneer in setting high standards for long-term care insurance.

Of 130 companies now marketing this product, only eight currently meet Massachusetts's relatively stringent criteria for licensing. Each company offers coverage in a variety of packages. But it is only the most extensive, and thus *expen*sive of these that offers reasonable protection against the staggering and *rising* cost of long-term care. Here's how that works:

Massachusetts requires that companies offer an optional inflation rider. That rider is critical. If you don't elect to take it, your coverage will be continually eroded by the rising cost of living. You will have to pay tomorrow's inflated bills with today's devalued dollars. Since most people who go into a nursing home are in their mid-eighties, the younger you are when you buy a policy, the more important is inflation protection. If you are buying a policy at a relatively young age in order to fix a lower rate you may not be needing benefits for many years, by which time inflation (which rises at a compounded rate) will have greatly diminished your benefits.

Unfortunately, even the most generous rider available in Massachusetts lags well behind the actual rate of increase in medical care costs. That means that the policyholder's benefits diminish every year. Only a tiny fraction of companies offer inflation riders that are compounded annually, a substantial consideration. Let's say at age 65 you buy a policy that pays $100 a day, for three years of care in a nursing home, with an inflation rider. In ten years you are institutionalized for two and a half years. Your bill at that time would be about

$200,000 at the current rate of inflation.

You will receive a net $120,000 in benefits, but you may still have to make up $80,000 out-of-pocket for a bed in an average (nothing fancy) nursing home.

Ethical issues and logistics aside, nursing home insurance doesn't financially put you ahead of the option of moving your assets, waiting thirty months, "greasing the skids" with cash to the nursing home and applying for Medicaid. What it *has* done is allow you to maintain full control of your assets.

Insurance companies tailor their policies to the regulations in each state. Therefore, this example may not work out the same way in your state. The costs and benefits may be different, but the problems will be the same. Wherever you live, if you buy a policy without inflation protection, your coverage will effectively shrink every year. With non-compounded inflation protection it still diminishes, but not as much.

Another consideration regarding coverage: Some companies tout their home care coverage as a way for you to use your benefits at home so that you won't need to go into a nursing home. According to Dr. James Firman of United Seniors Health

Cooperative, which participated in a study of the home care component of nursing home insurance, "For most people, the home care coverage won't cover much of anything. Don't buy this kind of policy if your purpose is to stay out of a nursing home. There are so many restrictions and technicalities in these policies that there would be only a small fraction of the total home care need that people would be able to collect on." Some of the newer and better policies have begun offering home care benefits, but like all other aspects of LTC insurance, it's buyer beware.

As a general rule, with nursing home insurance you get what you pay for. The best coverage is expensive, $2,000 a year and up. The more affordable policies generally offer only partial protection. According to Ron Pollack, of Families USA Foundation, "Even the most expensive of these policies have shortcomings that limit the protection you get. The cheapest have truly worrisome limitations."

The Traps

Restrictions and technicalities are the *other* big problem with nursing home insurance. *Consumer*

Reports in May 1988 published an article entitled "Who can afford a nursing home?" This 11-page survey of nursing home insurance stated: "We'd like to report that private insurance policies can meet the increasingly urgent need for long-term care coverage at a moderate cost. But many of the insurance policies we looked at were very expensive, severely limited in their coverage, or both... People who shop for them will run into a crazy quilt of charges, waivers, and limitations that confuse even insurance agents who sell the policies."

A storm of public protest over these policies has led to some reforms. In an attempt to curtail the worst abuses, the National Association of Insurance Commissioners (NAIC) drafted a model law and regulations that have been adopted in some form by most states. In some states, many unfair practices have been outlawed and companies not complying are barred from doing business. Other states have adopted weaker versions of the changes.

You can call your state Division of Insurance (see chart 10 page 258) to find out whether your state has adopted some form of the law or regulation. Ask if a summary of the regulation or the regulation itself is available and get the names of those companies that are approved to market long-term care policies in your state. When shopping for insurance, ask the agent to give you a sample policy, not just the promotional brochure *about* the policy. If there is any point on which you are confused by the language of the policy, ask for a clarification in writing.

Although the NAIC reforms are helpful to those who are shopping for a policy, approximately 800,000 people are currently paying for old, potentially useless policies they bought before the regulations went into effect. The regulations are *not* retroactive. If you purchased a policy before your state adopted the new regulations, it's time to review your policy before you pay another dime in premiums. By the way, in states without the new guidelines, many insurance companies are still selling the old, virtually worthless policies.

In October 1989, *Consumer Reports* printed a second article entitled "Paying for a Nursing Home," which spotlighted yet another problem presently being scrutinized by the National Association of Insurance Commissioners — the practice of "post-claims underwriting." Many insurance companies make a practice of waiting until you make a claim to determine your fitness for coverage — and it's legal. What that means is this: You might put in a claim as much as two years after you began paying for your policy and be told, "Sorry, you're not eligible because you didn't disclose that condition when we sold you the policy." The condition might have occurred some years ago — before the period you were asked to disclose. Nevertheless, you could still be ineligible. Or, your claim might be refused if you told the agent who sold you the policy about the condition and he neglected to write it down. (He has an incentive to be forgetful about marginal conditions that might disqualify you because he gets a big commission on the sale, up to the whole first year's premium.) Or, you might be denied benefits even if the illness that put you in the nursing home was unrelated to the one you didn't disclose.

There are a number of other disqualifying subtleties insurance companies use to keep you from collecting on your claim. *Consumer Reports'* conclusion: "It's impossible to know in advance how an insurance company will behave when you need to file a claim on a long-term care policy. Until more claims have been filed, and until insurance regulators make public the records of companies engaging in post-claims underwriting, you must protect yourself."

One way to do this is to be scrupulously thorough and honest in answering all questions on the application form. Don't even think about hiding any medical problem, big or small. Double check the application after the agent fills it out to be sure there are no errors or omissions. Any of these might later be used by the company to rescind your coverage.

A company that examines your medical history and requires an attending physician's statement before issuing the policy may be less likely to practice post-claims underwriting. Companies that issue a policy within a very short period of time may be more likely to later disqualify your claim when they take the time to scrutinize your medical history.

Post claims underwriting is just one problem standing in the way of getting your claim paid. Another is your insurance company might not be around when you go into a nursing home. In the past two years, 73 life and health insurers have gone belly up. An A rating (the second highest, after A+) from A.M.Best, the leading authority on insurance company finances, is no guarantee of stability. One failure, Farwest American, bore that rating until just before it collapsed.

In June, 1991, *Consumer Reports* took yet another look at long-term care policies. If anything, this time their assessment was even bleaker. In this excellent 17-page report entitled "The Traps in Long-Term Care Insurance," *CR* again assailed the insurance industry for the restrictive nature of their policies despite the NAIC regulations now in place. As one loophole in coverage was closed, another opened.

Other problems detailed by *Consumer Reports*:

• Lying or just plain ignorant agents. "Every sales agent misrepresented some aspect of the policy, the financial condition of the insurer, or the quality of the competitor's product. Not one sales agent properly explained the benefits, restrictions and policy limitations."

• The possibility of across-the-board rate increases which would force many people to drop their policies with no "nonforfeiture benefit" – meaning they get nothing back. "We believe large rate increases may be in store for many policy holders."

• Insufficient or absent regulation which *Consumer Reports* calls "Regulatory Roulette." "State regulators are overwhelmed by the sheer number of policies, their many themes and variations, and by the lack of staff to sort them all out...If the NAIC fails to act, Congress should make long-term care insurance work better for consumers..."

Despite all the problems, long-term care insurance is a terrific idea in theory because it allows you maximum control of your financial destiny. This type of insurance is useful primarily for people with substantial assets to protect, enough discretionary income to easily cover the premiums, and anxiety about the possibility of institutionalization.

When you are considering purchasing a policy, you must weigh all the factors that are specific to your own situation. An insurance agent is *not* an unbiased resource for helping you make a decision. If you are on a tight budget, it's probably not for you.

If you decide that long-term care insurance is a good option for you, don't buy until you thoroughly educate yourself. Some tips: Think twice before choosing a policy from anything less than an A+

rated company. Send for the NAIC booklet entitled "A Shopper's Guide to Long-Term Care" (see Resources). Make a trip to your local library to read the *Consumer Reports* articles discussed above, preferably all three. Especially, check the latest one for information and ratings of various policies. Or, to order a reprint of this article, see Resources, page 268.

Another informative article you can get from your local library is from the magazine, *New Choices*, June 1991. The writer's suggestion: "Here's another option for those considering long term care insurance: wait. Further regulatory reform is likely. So are better benefits... Of course waiting does entail risk. Some people find themselves in a nursing home at 60. But the biggest risk of all is buying without carefully examining all your options."

Better policies will include provisions for using benefits in other ways, such as an alternative care plan and/or home care. For example, a policy holder and his family are allowed to present a plan of care to the insurance company that permits the individual to stay at home and still receive benefits.

Another improvement would be some money back

(nonforfeiture benefits) paid upon cancellation after a certain period of time. Absent that, before you buy a policy, be sure you can afford to make the payments over a long period of time, even if there is an increase in the premium at a later date. Insurance companies are allowed to raise rates for a whole class of people even though they can't single you out for an increase. If you have to drop the policy because you can no longer afford it, without nonforfeiture benefits you will receive nothing back.

A word about group policies: They tend to be less expensive, however, most are unregulated by the states. There are *some* innovative group policies being developed that may hold *some* promise for solving *some* of the drawbacks in the long-term care area. But be very careful. Do not buy on price alone.

CHAPTER 9

NEGOTIATING WITH A NURSING HOME

For many people, the single most difficult decision they ever make is to put a parent or spouse into a nursing home. The decision always feels wrong. When the choice becomes unavoidable, it is made with guilt, sadness, and a sense of failure.

At such a time, you are emotionally unprepared to negotiate with a nursing home. Rather than shopping around to find the fairest price and researching the best services, the most you may be able to handle is one simple question: "Do you have a bed for my father?"

It's difficult enough to cope with the illness, let alone to investigate nursing homes. This chapter can't make the decision any less painful for you but it can help you understand how nursing homes operate and give you some tools to help you plan.

The nursing home's agenda

You are in a better position to evaluate nursing homes if you understand something about how their finances operate. Nursing homes generally are paid by three sources: cash, Medicaid and nursing home insurance. By far, the two most common forms of payment are cash and Medicaid. In most states, well over 60% of the nursing home population is on Medicaid.

With few exceptions, the rate for private pay patients is much higher than Medicaid's rate — as much as twice as high. Nursing homes are reimbursed by Medicaid through a complex formula based on several factors, such as the age of the facility, level of care, location, and capital improvements. Medicaid builds a small profit into the rate it pays nursing homes. Their real profits come from those who pay privately.

Though the demand for beds exceeds the supply, nursing homes are not making the killing that many people think they are. Their costs for labor are high, especially in urban areas. Capital improvements to bring the facilities up to code are expensive. Any unanticipated problems, such as a delay in Medicaid reimbursement, can make the difference between survival and bankruptcy.

That's why there has been a major shake-out in the nursing home industry in recent years. Small independent operators, usually undercapitalized, have been forced to sell out to the large national chains. But even the large corporations find it difficult to make a go of it, especially in states which, because of their own money problems, do not reimburse promptly.

A perfect example is Massachusetts. In 1989, the legislature was forced to raise the income tax rate 15 percent to pay off an estimated $800 million in back Medicaid costs. Some bills to nursing homes were outstanding for as long as eight years!

Because of financial pressures, nursing homes try to avoid taking Medicaid applicants. The problem is so acute that every state and the federal government has a book full of rules prohibiting discrimination against Medicaid applicants.

Nevertheless, discrimination does occur every day.

The last thing you want to do is to make a speech to a nursing home about how it's illegal to discriminate against your parent or spouse. You do want to approach the nursing home from a position of strength. Strength means money.

Your agenda

The rest of this chapter is useless to you unless you understand that you have to spend money to secure a bed in a good nursing home, even money that could be protected by following the steps we have covered in this book. In the real world, you have to buy your way into a nursing home. Average cost of the ticket: six to nine months private pay.

Here's how to find and get a bed in a good nursing home:

At least three to four months before an anticipated nursing home placement, begin researching your options. The factors to consider when evaluating a facility are: location, level of care provided, quality and cost.

Location

No decision about location should be made until all members of the family have been consulted. Which relatives will be visiting most often? Is there access to transportation? How close are other medical facilities such as hospitals?

Level of Care Provided

The ill person should be evaluated by the appropriate state or local authorities to determine the level of care required. Usually, the higher the level number, the less care necessary. A level III patient is generally able to look after himself with moderate assistance. A level II patient is generally bedridden and in need of constant custodial care. A level I patient requires continuing medical attention.

If the patient is going in on a private-pay basis at a more independent level of care (such as level III), make absolutely certain that the facility also takes at least level II patients. Some nursing homes, upon finding out that there are no more private funds, suddenly reclassify patients. If the facility does not provide the level of care needed, they can legitimately dump the patient.

Even though this may be wrong, the last thing you want is to get into an argument.

Quality of Care

The best way to find a good nursing home is to check with your local Council on Aging, state department of elderly affairs (if any), private groups such as Alzheimer's and Parkinson's support organizations, or a hospital social worker.

Costs

You should be the one to interview the nursing home about money, not the other way around. Find out what the costs are and the price of extras such as laundry, doctors' visits, and medications. Make sure that the facility is Medicaid certified. Find out what the policy is on when payment is due. Most states do not allow a nursing home to ask for a lump sum up front. If the subject comes up, don't make a speech about it, just suggest that the state may not allow it. (The objective is to find a bed for a person who desperately needs care, not start a lawsuit.)

Keep in mind that the nursing home wants to be sure there are private funds available. Therefore, you almost never get an answer to your question about bed availability until the nursing home gets an answer about who will pay. A commitment for a certain number of months of private pay is usually necessary to secure a bed.

LEGAL INSTRUMENTS

This chapter shows you how assets can be handled if you know that at some time in the future you will not be able to manage your own financial affairs. It is also for people who are making arrangements for friends or relatives who cannot presently handle their financial affairs.

The power of attorney – regular and durable

A power of attorney is a legal instrument that gives to another or others the right to handle financial affairs. Typically, a person will create a power of attorney to give another the right to have access to a bank account or to sell stock on his behalf. The person given this responsibility does not have to be an attorney.

A **regular power of attorney** usually gives specific and limited powers like the ones mentioned above. It usually does not have an expiration date but ceases the minute you become incapacitated.

A **durable power of attorney** is exactly the same except that it remains valid even if you become incapacitated. It can be very effective in planning to protect assets which otherwise would have to be spent on a nursing home.

Example: Peter is a widower with two children. He has $50,000 in cash and $10,000 in stock in his name only. His wife recently died in a nursing home. He is concerned about protecting his assets if he needs long-term care but does not want to give up control while he is still healthy.

Peter could simply put his children's names on his assets. However, if one of his children gets divorced or gets into financial trouble, his assets could be in jeopardy.

Or he could make up a durable power of attorney giving authority to one or both offspring to get at his assets should he become incapacitated. If he became ill and couldn't get at his assets, let alone manage them, his children could use the power of attorney to close out the accounts and transfer the assets to their names.

Warning: Giving a power of attorney is giving away control. It is not advisable to do this unless absolutely necessary. It is best to give it to someone who is trustworthy to hold *until it is needed*. Instructions should be given about how and when it will be used.

If your state allows it, consider putting two people on the power of attorney so there are checks and balances.

Consider a "springing" durable power of attorney. This instrument is valid only when you become incapacitated, unlike a regular or durable power of attorney which becomes effective the moment you sign.

Make sure you update! The biggest mistake lawyers and financial advisors make when recommending powers of attorney is to forget to inform their clients that most financial institutions will not accept them after a period of time. There is no set policy on when the instrument becomes "stale." Remember, a power of attorney is only as good as a person's or institution's willingness to accept it. Update by rewriting it (if only by changing the effective date) at least every two years.

Conservatorships

A conservatorship usually means that a person has requested of an appropriate court permission to handle the assets and affairs of someone who is incapacitated (the ward). Anyone can be named a conservator. In some states the ward can participate in choosing a conservator.

Once a person is appointed by the court, she becomes responsible for handling the assets in approximately the same way the ward would. Conservatorships are almost useless in protecting assets unless the ward has at least 30 months to plan to protect countable assets.

A durable power of attorney would be just as effective as a conservatorship at a fraction of the cost and without having the court and the world know your business.

Conservatorships are most effective when a person becomes so ill that long-term management of his/her assets is necessary. Readers of this book who have acted on what they learned should not find this alternative attractive or necessary.

Those with relatives who are already ill and who may need a nursing home down the road may think that a conservatorship is the answer. The problem is that Medicaid planning, in practice, means taking the assets out of the ward's name. A conservatorship, by definition, means keeping the assets in the ward's name but under the legal control of the conservator. Therefore, a conservator never gets assets away from Medicaid, but rather *preserves them* for Medicaid

Conservatorships therefore should not be considered until you consult with an attorney who understands Medicaid.

Guardianships

A guardianship is the same as a conservatorship except that the court grants to the guardian control of the ward's body as well as his assets. The guardian requests that the court grant power to make decisions about such things as medication, treatment, and even matters of life and death.

On the subject of protecting assets, it is enough to say that a guardianship has the same advantages (not many) and disadvantages (many) as a conservatorship.

CHOOSING A LAWYER

Where to look for a lawyer

The practice of Medicaid law is a very specialized field. Few lawyers can speak its language fluently.

Here are some suggestions for finding an attorney with expertise in this field:

• Call your local council on aging or its equivalent for referrals.

• Speak to the social worker at your area hospital. Many have dealt with nursing home placement and are familiar with attorneys who work in the field.

• Speak to your doctor, but make sure he has worked on *Medicaid* issues with the attorney he recommends.

• An excellent source of experienced attorneys is local support groups like Alzheimer's, Parkinson's and stroke victims' organizations.

• If you have a family lawyer whom you trust, ask him to find a lawyer who concentrates in the elder law field.

• If you still can't get a name of a reputable elder law attorney, see page 274 for how to send away for names in your state.

Here are some suggestions on how not to find an attorney:

• Don't choose an attorney from an advertisement. Anyone can call himself an expert.

• Don't rely on your local bar association referral service. Few, if any, have a category that deals with this subject. If they deal with it at all, they lump the subject with estate planning. Estate planners do not necessarily understand Medicaid.

Interviewing a lawyer

Here are some points to raise with the attorney you are considering:

• What percentage of his practice is devoted to Medicaid law?

• Have him show you the specific regulations that cover Medicaid eligibility in your state. You'd be surprised how many lawyers don't have them.

• Ask if he has spoken or written on the subject.

• Ask him how he charges and specifically what work is performed. Make sure the attorney is willing to write you a comprehensive follow-up letter after your initial meeting. It is difficult to absorb everything the lawyer says in a first meeting.

The letter will clarify questions raised and will give you the maximum benefit from this book.

Here are some telling questions for interviewing lawyers:

"I'm a little confused about how SIA works in this state. Can you explain this to me?"

Any lawyer who hesitates or asks you what you mean doesn't belong in this field. The Spousal Impoverishment Act is considered basic Medicaid law.

"My mother is concerned that she'll lose her house if she goes into a nursing home. She wants to 'sell' it to me and and take a note from me for the purchase price. Is this a good idea?"

Basic Medicaid law dictates that you never take a non-countable asset, like a house, and convert it into a countable one, like money. Aside from the fact that you're creating an instant capital gains tax problem, the note that your mother holds could remain a countable asset for years.

"My father is becoming forgetful although he still mostly manages on his own. He has a house and $50,000. I'm concerned he may need a nursing home some day. Should I get a conservatorship?"

If the lawyer answers yes, get up and walk out. Conservators cannot shift assets without a court's permission The conservator's job is to preserve assets. Can you imagine going to a judge and saying that you want to protect your fathers assets by transferring them to yourself? Right!

The better answer from a lawyer is to suggest that you sit down with your father and explain that assets might be lost to a nursing home if he doesn't do some planning now and suggest that he take steps while he's well, such as shifting assets or setting up an irrevocable trust.

Mark up this book and take it with you when you go to see the attorney. That's what the wide margins are for. By now you have some idea of what needs to be done. Be prepared with a list of your own questions. Does the lawyer seem to know what he or she is talking about? You now have enough information to be a pretty good judge of a lawyer's expertise. If the answers you get make you uncomfortable, politely excuse yourself and find someone who knows more about the field of elder law.

CHAPTER 12

ESTATE PLANNING

Looking again at your estate planning

As people get older people, they often consult with a lawyer, accountant, or financial planner to set their affairs in order. They may write a will and take certain steps to avoid death taxes and costly probate procedures. Here's a caution however: If you have set up your estate simply to save death taxes, you could lose the whole ball of wax before anybody dies.

The problem is that estate planning deals with what will happen to your assets when you die. Good estate planning isn't necessarily good later life planning. With the life expectancy climbing past 80, and more and more people entering nursing homes, it's extremely important to plan for old age as well as death.

Medicaid, the only public program that pays for long-term care, is a law unto itself – one you and your advisor must understand before drafting an estate plan.

Smart estate planning can be disastrous if illness strikes

Many traditional techniques used in estate planning ignore the possibility that one or both spouses may need a nursing home at some time. For instance, basic estate planning would dictate that assets be divided between the husband and wife to minimize death taxes.

Your accountant may be under the impression that this strategy also protects assets from nursing home fees; he may assume that all the facility can get are the assets of the patient.

Wrong. Under Medicaid, all assets, regardless of whose name they are in, are joined together. Except for non-countable assets, everything is at risk, regardless of where it came from, who earned it, or whose name it's in.

Also vulnerable are assets in a second marriage, even with a prenuptial agreement. Medicaid does not recognize premarital agreements Even though the spouses have agreed to keep their assets separate, Medicaid joins them together, in effect ignoring the couple's wishes and subjecting the well spouse's assets to nursing home costs. Dividing assets is a mistake that could be devastating.

Another seemingly good estate planning idea: In the case of a couple where one spouse is not well, you might consider transferring the assets to the name of the healthy spouse to avoid death taxes. Putting aside gift tax considerations (both federal and state taxes may be applicable), there probably would be moderate savings in death taxes upon the demise of the ill spouse.

However, this idea gets you absolutely nowhere with Medicaid, should the ill spouse need a nursing home. All assets, regardless of whose name they are in, are joined together. Transferring assets to the healthy spouse does not keep them from the nursing home.

Another common estate plan is the establishing of trusts. If established correctly, a trust can save thousands of dollars in death taxes, particularly for the surviving spouse. However, if these trusts are set up incorrectly, all assets could also be available to Medicaid. Medicaid's position is that if the donors (typically Mom and Dad) reserve the right to get principal from a trustee (regardless of whether or not the trustee can say no), these monies would be available. Therefore, good estate planning could subject these assets to being spent on long-term care.

Another common device for minimizing death taxes is the sale of assets and the taking back of paper. In a typical situation, the parent would "sell" the property to the children and take back a note that represents the fair market value of the property. This debt would then be "forgiven" over a period of years. If the people who sold the property live long enough, there would be little or no assets to be taxed upon their death. The problem, of course, is that the note becomes a countable asset under Medicaid and would probably disqualify an applicant from eligibility.

As you can see, it's extremely important to look at your estate planning with the possibility of long-term care in mind. Speak with your financial advisor about these concerns; don't assume that he or she is aware of the problem. Traditional estate planning may save death taxes for middle class families, but it often conflicts with good Medicaid planning.

CHAPTER 13

A CONVERSATION ABOUT FINANCES BETWEEN THE GENERATIONS

Elderly parents and their adult children may love each other deeply yet be unable to communicate effectively on even the simplest matters. When big problems loom, communication can break down completely, leaving both sides hurt and miserable. More important, without good communication problems don't get handled in a timely fashion and complications ensue that could have been avoided. For both sides it is well worth the effort to work at keeping the lines open for a continuing dialog on important issues.

One way to do this is for parents and children to remember that they are the product of different major life experiences and different times and so each speaks a language that is foreign and often unintelligible to the other.

The parents' side

Anyone past the age of 60, still bears the scars of the most traumatic economic event in the twentieth century, the Great Depression. No one who has not experienced those desperate times can understand how they shape your thinking ever after.

Your children, wonderful as they are, have no idea what you went through to earn whatever nest egg you've managed to put together over the years. A depression to you means losing everything and being helpless to do anything about it. It scares you to death to think about it. A depression to your kids, it seems, is having to keep their car for more than three years.

As you get older, you face the possibility of another terrifying experience. Painful as memories of economic hard times may be, you have something even more difficult to deal with: the insidious loss of your independence as you get older. You may have survived the depression; you're not going to survive old age.

During your lifetime, you came to rely upon yourself and your good judgement about how to handle your money. Now you're beginning to sense that you may some day need to depend more and more on your children. That's a hard pill to swallow. Can you imagine asking your children for *their* advice about *your* money?

The painful fact you need to face now is that loss of independence, to one degree or another, is a common, and sometimes inevitable, part of the aging process. If you continue to delude yourself that nothing will ever change, not only will you risk losing your life savings but you may cause a great deal of pain to yourself and to your children in the process.

First, you must make the threshold decision: Do you trust your children? Have they done the right thing with their lives, their spouses and with you? You may not agree with how they spend their money, or they may not raise your grandchildren the way you would, but be honest with yourself: Are they happy? Do they genuinely care about you and respect what you've tried to do with your life?

If the answer is yes, then we move on to how you can communicate your concerns about losing control of your assets and your health. If the answer is no, you may need to look to others to help you.

You have always been there for your children; now it's time to consider having your children there for you. This is the truth: The legal and medical system that will affect you should you become seriously ill can be devastating if you are not prepared. Your children can be an enormous help in getting prepared. There is no better ally than a loyal and loving offspring in helping you maintain your independence.

Children want to help, but they're afraid to offend, they're frightened by what they see happening, but they don't know what to do. They are scared to death they're going to lose you and not be able to say to themselves that they were there to help. Your job now is to put aside a little of your fierce independence and enlist their support as you make your plans.

Step one: Bring them into the circle. Let them know about your health and your finances.

Step two: Ask for their opinion and respect it when it's offered.

Step three: Play out a series of scenarios concerning your health in the future and consider what finances will be necessary to pay.

Step four: Even if health issues are not a problem, discuss where you want to spend the rest of your life and what money will be necessary to make your hopes come true.

Step 5: Once you've established a working relationship with your children, seek professional financial and legal help, making sure your children are included.

The children's side

Legally, you are not financially at risk should your parents become seriously ill and need long-term care. When Congress reformed the Medicaid laws in 1988, the states were specifically prohibited from holding children responsible for the cost of their parents' care in a nursing home.

Although you may not legally be held responsible for your parents' medical bills, most adult children will make enormous financial sacrifices to assist their mother and father in their hour of need. So, to some extent, your security may also be at stake when you bring up these discussions and try to get your parents to make wise decisions now to protect themselves in the future.

More important, you want the best for your parents. You have some idea of the risks they face. What should you do?

A message on a Father's Day card speaks volumes about how we see our parents as we ourselves get on in years: "The older I get, the perfecter you were."

For most of us, our parents were generally right in how they raised us and how they handled their money. Although you may not have agreed with them and may not choose to raise your own kids as you were raised, you have probably reached the stage in your life where you respect them for what they tried to do.

Now you want to help them prepare for their later years and you don't know how to start. You want to discuss finances with them but the subject seems impossibly difficult. To make matters worse, they show little interest in hearing your opinions on what they should be doing about their future.

You're not going to change your parents! You need your head examined (if it already hasn't been) if you think you will. They sometimes drive you to distraction; they don't listen, they won't accept your help with anything. But that doesn't mean you should give up.

Don't confuse change with cooperation. Their stubbornness and your frustration may keep you apart. Just remember, you both have the same goals: their well-being.

Some suggestions for opening the lines of communication:

Step one: The way you state your concern is very important. Use "I" messages. For instance, "Mom, I worry that if there is a serious medical problem some day, we have not made any plans for handling it."

Let control stay with the parent: "If you're not able to mange on your own at some point, we would like to be able to assist. We need to know how you would like us to help you. Could we sit down and discuss finances so we can figure out how we should plan for the future?" Notice the emphasis is on your concern "I worry", while allowing Mom to keep control "how *you* would like us to help you."

If you meet with resistance, don't be discouraged. Wait awhile and bring up the subject again when the opportunity presents itself. Perhaps the most difficult thing is to apply subtle pressure over a period of time to convince them that steps must be taken to protect their assets. Keep raising the subject but don't nag. This stuff is hard for everyone to deal with.

Step two: Respect and try to understand what they're going through emotionally and physically as the aging process takes its toll. Don't lose your sense of humor. Keep a light touch. Be loving. Listen to their ideas with interest and respect.

Step three: Seek professional help – financial and/or legal. An accountant or lawyer familiar with Medicaid planning is invaluable at this time.

Remember: this is an adjustment period for all concerned. Coping with new problems can be difficult and frustrating. However, once you recognize that you have a problem, you can seek help. Start with good book or two. There are a number of fine self-help books for care givers and seniors that can ease some of the burdens and point everyone in the direction of additional help (see Resources, page 262).

If you are already dealing with a serious health condition, there are support groups for virtually any problem (see Resources, page 271). Even if you usually don't consider yourself a "joiner," this is the time to reach out for help. People who struggle in isolation with overwhelming burdens, run the risk of becoming ill themselves from the strain. Just having the opportunity to ventilate your frustrations in a safe and supportive atmosphere can be liberating.

Women, particularly, are prone to feeling that they must handle every problem themselves, sacrificing till they are stretched to the breaking point. Under stressful conditions, it's easy to lose one's perspective and sense of balance. A support group can be invaluable in providing tried and true advice and referrals from people who have been in the same boat.

Coping with the inexorable challenges of aging can leave us feeling helpless. The way to regain a feeling of being in control is by doing something. Get on the phone and network. Call your local council on aging or office of elder affairs. Call a hotline. Call anyone you know who has dealt with a similar problem. Keep asking questions till you get the information and help you need. It's surprising how many places there are that offer assistance, often for free, once you make the effort to search them out.

TAX CONSIDERATIONS

TAX CONSIDERATIONS

Any plan to protect assets from the cost of catastrophic illness generally involves taking assets out of your name. That can end up being a two-edged sword: you may protect assets from a nursing home only to make them available to the federal or state government because of poor tax planning. This chapter sets forth a summary of current tax law as it applies to asset transfers. It is not intended as the final word on tax strategy — that is left to your financial advisor.

In order to take into consideration the effect of taxes on your plan, you need to be familiar with certain terms and concepts. Here they are:

Once-in-a-lifetime exemption from capital gains tax

Section 121 of the Internal Revenue Code allows homeowners who are 55 or older, and who meet certain ownership and residence requirements, to exclude from taxation up to a maximum of $125,000 of gain (net profit) from the sale of their principal residence.

To qualify, only one of the parties needs to be 55 and the home must be used as a principal residence for three out of the five years prior to the sale. If a homeowner resides in a nursing home or long-term care facility, the residency requirement is reduced to one year.

Stepped-up basis

The world of capital gains tax revolves around two points: what you paid for something and what you get when you sell it. What you paid for an asset is called a basis. The basis can be increased in many instances by adding in the cost of major improvements. For instance, if you paid $20,000 for your house and sold it for $100,000 (net the expenses in selling it) the capital gain is $80,000. If you had spent $10,000 for a new roof and kitchen, your basis would be $30,000 or a $70,000 gain when you sell. You pay taxes on the gain.

If assets are in your name when you die, their basis increases (gets "stepped-up") to the fair market value if a death tax return is filed. Assuming your children inherit the assets and sell them immediately, they will incur no capital gains tax. *Example: Roy Parker has a house currently worth $100,000 and stock worth $50,000. He paid $10,000 for the house and $5,000 for the stock. If he sells* *everything during his life, he will have a capital gain of $135,000. If he dies with the assets in his name, assuming his offspring fills out a death tax return, the basis of $15,000 gets "stepped up" to the values placed on the return. If that figure is $150,000 and the offspring immediately sells it, there will be no capital gains.*

Rollover of taxable gains

Under section 1034 of the Internal Revenue Code, if you sell your home and reinvest any gain you receive in a house of equal or greater value within two years, you do not have to pay taxes on your gain. This is called a "rollover" and it allows you to trade up to a better house any number of times without incurring capital gains tax at each sale. If you buy a less expensive house, you would have to pay tax on whatever portion of your gain you do not reinvest.

Transfer of assets

1) To a spouse

There are no tax consequences on transfers between spouses. Section 1041 of the Internal Revenue Code provides that there is no taxable gain to either party unless the person receiving the property is a non-resident alien. There is also no tax consequence if transfers are made as part of a divorce settlement. The basis of the property transferred remains the same.

2) To children

Transfers to a child have the same tax consequences as transfers between spouses with two important exceptions: The total joint assets of the parents making the transfers must be under $1.2 million ($600,000 if one parent) and the child picks up the parents' basis.

Outright gifts/transfers

There is a great deal of confusion about the issue of federal gift tax. Many people think that they can only give away (transfer) up to $10,000 a year per person, ($20,000 per couple) without having to pay a gift tax.

That's only partially accurate. True, gifts under $10,000 a year are not subject to gift tax. Yearly gifts over $10,000 per person are subject to taxes but the government gives you a credit against them. The maximum credit is $192,800 which represents the tax on a gift of $600,000. Double both of those figures for a couple. This same credit is also available to be used to offset taxes on your estate when you die. That's why it's called the "unified credit against gift and death tax." A person dying with assets of $600,000 or less would incur a tax but it would be offset by the credit. If your estate is over $600,000 you might want to give away some of your assets now so all of the credit would be available to be used against your death tax. That's why people with assets over $600,000 ($1.2 million per couple) give away gifts of less that $10,000 annually. If your assets are under $600,000, you can give away as much as you want in a singe year. It doesn't really matter since the tax on both your gifts and what's left in your estate when you die will always be less than your credit.

Tax considerations in establishing:

1) An irrevocable trust

An irrevocable trust is similar to a revocable trust in that the purpose of both is to hold assets. The difference is that the person (donor) who establishes the irrevocable trust gives up control and ownership completely. In a revocable trust, although ownership is given up, full control is maintained meaning that the donor has the power to modify or terminate the trust at any time.

Irrevocable trusts are taxed as separate taxpayers on any income not distributed to beneficiaries during the year. Great care must be taken if this type of trust is to be used since it is likely that all income, gain, loss, deductions and credits would apply only to the trust and not to the individual. If, for example, you place your primary residence in an irrevocable trust and it was later sold, you would not, in most cases, be able to claim the once-in-a-lifetime $125,000 exemption from capital gains tax.

2) A revocable trust

These are also referred to as "grantor" or "donor" trusts. Since the person establishing them maintains the right to terminate or modify them, these instruments do not exist for tax purposes. Therefore, any income, loss, gain, deduction or credit would stay with the person who established the trust.

3) A life estate

A life estate is an outright transfer of a person's home or other real estate with one provision: The person transferring the property, typically parents, reserve the right to live in the property for their lifetime, collect any rental income, pay taxes and take deductions. In short, they have a "life interest" in that property. Best of all, the property avoids a Medicaid lien.

The children, although they have ownership, cannot sell, mortgage, rent, or evict the life tenant.

These are the the tax benefits:

1) The parent(s) can deduct expenses and claim any income on their tax return. The children have no tax obligation.

2) The property goes through their taxable estate upon the parents' deaths, which means the basis gets "stepped up" (see above).

These are the tax disadvantages:

1) Elderly people often qualify for an abatement (decrease) of their real estate taxes. Any abatement of real estate taxes is lost.

2) The person transferring the property loses the once-in-a-lifetime $125,000 exemption from capital gains tax.

3) The property no longer qualifies for rollover treatment under Section 1034 of the Internal Revenue Code.

4) The property may be vulnerable to lawsuits brought against the children who now own it or be subject to being divided if a child gets divorced.

Deductibility of nursing home expenses

Many people enter a nursing home as private-pay patients. Although they may not be eligible for Medicaid, they may be able to save on their income taxes by deducting their medical expenses. In order to qualify as a legitimate deduction under Internal Revenue Code 213, expenses for medical care must exceed 7.5 percent of the taxpayer's adjusted gross income.

If a physician states that a primary reason for institutionalization was the need for medical care, then all nursing home expenses, not just the medical portion are deductible. If a person is in a nursing home for custodial care, rather than strictly medical care, he may not be able to deduct the cost of his meals and lodging but could deduct whatever expenses were medical in nature.

When taking tax deductions for medical expenses, you need to keep good records of all expenses. These may include statements from doctors, bills for treatments, medications, transportation, eyeglasses and hearing aids, medical insurance premiums, etc.

Dependency exemption

If an institutionalized person has transferred assets to a child, the child may find it necessary to pay the nursing home bill for a period of time. Often the child can claim a dependency exemption for the parent (or grandparent, for that matter). Or, if there are several relatives helping out with expenses, the exemption and deductions can be allocated among them.

In order to qualify as a dependent, a person must receive less than $2,000 of gross income per taxable year and meet the following criteria which the IRS uses to define a dependent:

1) Over half of the dependent's support for the year was provided by the person claiming the exemption

2) The dependent is a U.S. citizen

3) The dependent did not file a joint return

4) The dependent is related to the taxpayer

LIVING WILLS

Who decides what happens to you?

Putting aside the issue of pain and suffering to the patient, there is no surer and less productive way to run through your life savings than to be kept alive for an interminable period of time when you are desperately ill with no possibility of recovery. This issue concerns not only you, but also your family. The possibility of weeks, months, even years of dehumanizing invasive procedures and artificial life support systems administered to no avail is terrifying to all concerned. If you want to lessen the risk that this scenario will ever happen to you, you should plan ahead now.

Let's examine the issue of who makes decisions for a hopelessly ill, mentally incompetent person by considering a typical case:

Malcolm suffers a severe heart attack, the third such crisis in a year. His brain has been deprived of oxygen and although he may not survive for long, for the rest of his life he will be virtually brain-dead and need life support systems.

Over the years, he has expressed to his family that if something serious ever happened to him he would not want to go on living "like a vegetable."

Question: Which of the following people can make a decision about continuing life support to prolong Malcolm's life ?

1) his wife
2) his adult children from his first marriage
3) his 17-year-old child from the current wife
4) his parents
5) his brothers and sisters
6) his doctor
7) the hospital administrator
8) his lawyer

Get the point?!?

The fact is none of these people can make the decision, only Malcolm can, and therein lies the reason that so many people in this country are now interested in a thing called a living will.

Who makes life and death decisions for a person who is irreversibly mentally and physically incompetent and unable to choose for himself? Ideally, the patient, at a time when his mental faculties are sound.

Because of the notoriety of the Karen Ann Quinlan and Nancy Cruzan cases, this question has emerged as a burning issue in recent months. The problem has implications for all of us.

In the case of Cruzan v. Director, Missouri Department of Health, in June 1990 the Supreme Court ruled that Nancy Cruzan, a young patient in a persistent vegetative state (an irreversible coma) had to be artificially kept alive because she had not shown through documents or actions clearly and convincingly that she would want such measures discontinued. The Supreme Court stated that if Nancy Cruzan had made her wishes known when she was well, they would have been honored.

That's the idea behind a living will. A living will, also called an advance directive, is your statement to the world defining your wishes should you become profoundly ill and irreversibly incompetent and need life support systems or heroic measures to keep you alive. It spells out to all concerned what measures may be taken, and what not, so that you may be allowed to die with dignity and without unwanted intervention.

A living will does not direct someone to end your life. Its purpose is to prevent the medical establishment and anyone else from keeping you alive through the use of artificial methods and continued heroic efforts.

If you were to become incompetent, the usual criteria for determining whether or not extraordinary methods would be used on you is whether there was any possibility of your returning to a degree of consciousness where you would be able to interact meaningfully with your family and to partake in the pleasures of living.

Are living wills legal? The truth is that you have the constitutional and common law right to refuse treatment you do not want, assuming you are mentally competent at the time you make these decisions. Most states now have living will laws, but even if yours does not, such a document is still an excellent protection because it gives the court a clear indication of what your wishes are.

Potential problems

The following points should be dealt with *before* you sign a living will:

1) You must discuss your wishes and the reasons behind them with your family. Even with a living

will, if a family member objects to your directives, it may be necessary for a court to review your situation. By discussing the matter with family and friends, you are creating potential witnesses to support your mental capacity and reasons for executing the instrument. Give key family members and friends copies of the signed document.

2) You may chose a person whom you trust to be your "proxy" to make decisions for you should you lose your mental faculties. Think very carefully about your choice to hold this power. Make sure he/she is sympathetic to your point of view and strong enough to stand up for it. Have your proxy come with you when you speak with your doctor.

3) A living will has limitations. For instance, you may specify that you do not wish to have your heart started mechanically if it stops beating. You also may not wish to receive such procedures as tube feeding and hydration. If that is your wish, you must specifically include language that covers food and water administered artificially. Not all states honor directives against tube feeding, but you have a better chance of getting your way if you spell it out clearly.

4) A recent study found that doctors don't follow their patients' directives about a quarter of the time, sometimes because the living will was missing from the patient's chart. Another study found that many doctors aren't themselves comfortable about discussing the topic with their patients. If your doctor hasn't brought the matter up, don't be shy. Take the initiative and tell your doctor what your wishes are and give him a copy of the signed document. Another copy should be held by your lawyer.

To obtain more information on living wills, advance medical directives and a sample document for your state, see Resources, page 261.

CHAPTER 16

The Charts

The following charts have been compiled from extensive surveys of state welfare offices and attorneys who specialize in Medicaid and estate planning. Every effort has been made to assure their accuracy. However, regulations in various states are subject to interpretation and therefore these charts are to be used as a guideline only.

Chart 1

1991 Community Spouse Resource Allowance Limit

This chart shows the limit on countable assets each state allows the stay-at-home (community) spouse to keep. Federal law permits each state to set a figure anywhere between a minimum of $13,296 and a maximum of $66,480. The amount goes up yearly.

State	Amount		State	Amount
Alabama	$25,000		Montana	13,296
Alaska	62,480		Nebraska	66,480
Arizona	66,480		Nevada	13,296
Arkansas	60,000		New Hampshire	13,296
California	66,480		New Jersey	13,296
Colorado	66,480		New Mexico	31,290
Connecticut	66,480		New York	66,480
Delaware	13,296		North Carolina	66,480
District of Columbia	66,480		North Dakota	25,000
Florida	66,480		Ohio	13,296
Georgia	66,480		Oklahoma	66,480
Hawaii	62,480		Oregon	13,296
Idaho	66,480		Pennsylvania	13,296
Illinois	66,480		Rhode Island	13,296
Indiana	66,462		South Carolina	66,480
Iowa	24,000		South Dakota	62,580
Kansas	66,480		Tennessee	13,296
Kentucky	66,480		Texas	13,296
Louisiana	66,480		Utah	13,296
Maine	66,480		Vermont	66,480
Maryland	66,480		Virginia	13,296
Massachusetts	13,296		Washington	66,480
Michigan	13,296		West Virginia	13,296
Minnesota	13,296		Wisconsin	66,480
Mississippi	66,480		Wyoming	66,480
Missouri	13,296			

Chart 1   241

Chart 2

States where you can qualify for Medicaid as long your monthly income is less than your monthly nursing home bill

California	Nebraska
Connecticut	New Hampshire
District of Columbia	New York
Hawaii	North Carolina
Illinois	North Dakota
Indiana	Oregon
Kansas	Pennsylvania
Kentucky	Rhode Island
Maine	Utah
Maryland	Vermont
Massachusetts	Virginia
Michigan	Washington
Minnesota	Wisconsin
Missouri	
Montana	

Chart 3

Cap States
States with a limit on how much monthly income
a person can have and still qualify for Medicaid

State	Income Limit	State	Income Limit
Alabama	$1,221	Mississippi	1,221
Alaska	1,221	Nevada	1,221
Arizona	1,221	New Jersey	1,221
Arkansas	1,221	New Mexico	1,043
Colorado	1,221	Oklahoma	1,221
Delaware	875	South Carolina	1,221
Florida	1,221	South Dakota	1,221
Georgia	1,221	Tennessee	1,221
Idaho	1,221	Wyoming	1,221
Iowa	1,221	West Virginia	1,221
Louisiana	1,221	Ohio	1,221

Chart 3   243

Chart 4

What a state allows a person to keep monthly for personal needs

This chart applies to the nursing home resident only and tells how much monthly income can be put aside for personal needs.

State	Amount	State	Amount
Alabama	$30	Montana	$40
Alaska	75	Nebraska	35
Arizona	61.05	Nevada	35
Arkansas	30	New Hampshire	40
California	35	New Jersey	35
Colorado	34	New Mexico	40
Connecticut	42	New York	40
Delaware	36	North Carolina	30
District of Columbia	60	North Dakota	45
Florida	35	Ohio	30
Georgia	30	Oklahoma	30
Hawaii	30	Oregon	30
Idaho	30	Pennsylvania	30
Illinois	30	Rhode Island	40
Indiana	30	South Carolina	30
Iowa	30	South Dakota	30
Kansas	30	Tennessee	30
Kentucky	40	Texas	30
Louisiana	38	Utah	30
Maine	40	Vermont	30
Maryland	40	Virginia	30
Massachusetts	65	Washington	41.62
Michigan	32	West Virginia	30
Minnesota	49	Wisconsin	40
Mississippi	44	Wyoming	30

Chart 5

Income limits for the stay-at-home spouse

This chart shows the maximum amount of __joint__ income allowed the at-home spouse of a Medicaid applicant. This information only applies if the at-home spouse's income is less than the amounts below. The at-home spouse's income (if any) plus a portion of the institutionalized spouse's income can add up to no more than the amounts below. The stay-at-home spouse has no obligation to contribute any of his/her own income to the institutionalized spouse, even if that income exceeds the limits below.

Alabama	$856	Montana	1,662
Alaska	1,565	Nebraska	903
Arizona	1,662	Nevada	1,662
Arkansas	856	New Hampshire	1,662
California	1,662	New Jersey	1,662
Colorado	1,662	New Mexico	903
Connecticut	1,662	New York	1,662
Delaware	1,662	North Carolina	1,662
District of Columbia	1,662	North Dakota	1,662
Florida	1,662	Ohio	984
Georgia	1,662	Oklahoma	1,662
Hawaii	1,565	Oregon	856
Idaho	1,662	Pennsylvania	1,662
Illinois	1,662	Rhode Island	985
Indiana	1,662	South Carolina	1,662
Iowa	1,662	South Dakota	1,565
Kansas	1,662	Tennessee	1,662
Kentucky	1,662	Texas	1,662
Louisiana	1,662	Utah	856
Maine	1,662	Vermont	1,200
Maryland	1,662	Virginia	1,662
Massachusetts	1,662	Washington	1,662
Michigan	1,662	West Virginia	1,662
Minnesota	1,662	Wisconsin	1,662
Mississippi	1,662	Wyoming	1,662
Missouri	1,662		

Chart 5   245

Chart 6

Maximum amount of cash that can be kept by a person entering a nursing home

Alabama	$2,000	Montana	N/A
Alaska	2,000	Nebraska	1,600
Arizona	2,000	Nevada	2,000
Arkansas	2,000	New Hampshire	2,500
California	2,000	New Jersey	2,000
Colorado	2,000	New Mexico	2,000
Connecticut	1,600	New York	3,000
Delaware	2,000	North Carolina	1,500
District of Columbia	2,600	North Dakota	3,000
Florida	2,000	Ohio	1,500
Georgia	2,000	Oklahoma	2,000
Hawaii	2,000	Oregon	2,000
Idaho	2,000	Pennsylvania	2,400
Illinois	2,000	Rhode Island	4,000
Indiana	1,500	South Carolina	2,000
Iowa	2,000	South Dakota	2,000
Kansas	2,000	Tennessee	2,000
Kentucky	2,000	Texas	2,000
Louisiana	2,000	Utah	2,000
Maine	2,000	Vermont	2,000
Maryland	2,500	Virginia	2,000
Massachusetts	2,000	Washington	2,000
Michigan	2,000	West Virginia	2,000
Minnesota	3,000	Wisconsin	2,000
Mississippi	2,000	Wyoming	2,000
Missouri	999.99		

Chart 7

Requirements for protecting your house from a nursing home

The states are reimbursed half of their Medicaid expenses by the federal government. The government has its own regulations for Medicaid eligibility that they encourage the states to adopt but do not make mandatory.

One such regulation deals with re-classifying a person's house (primary residence) from a non-countable to a countable asset. Under these federal guidelines, if a single person is in a nursing home for more than a certain period of time, the state has a right to terminate its non-countable status and force the sale of the property to pay the bill. This chart shows you which states have adopted this option.

Your house is protected if you have:

	An intent to return to the house	A doctor's certificate that you are expected to return	Even if you do not return to the house	Time limit on protection?
Alabama	✔	✔	✔	NONE
Alaska	✔			NONE
Arkansas	✔			NONE
Arizona	✔			NONE
California	✔			NONE
Colorado	✔			NONE
Connecticut		✔		NONE
Delaware	✔			NONE
District of Columbia	✔			NONE
Florida[1]	✔			NONE

Chart 7   247

Chart 7 continued

Requirements for protecting your house house from a nursing home

	An intent to return to the house	A doctor's certificate that you are expected to return	Even if you do not return to the house	Time limit on protection?
Georgia	✔			NONE
Hawaii	✔			NONE
Idaho	✔			NONE
Illinois	✔			NONE
Indiana	✔			NONE
Iowa	✔			
Kansas	✔			NONE
Kentucky			✔	NONE
Louisiana	✔			NONE
Maine	✔			NONE
Maryland	✔	✔		NONE
Massachusetts[2]			✔	NONE
Michigan			✔	NONE
Minnesota			✔	6 mos.
Mississippi				NONE
Missouri			✔	NONE
Montana		✔		6 mos.
Nebraska		✔		6 mos.
Nevada		✔		NONE
New Hampshire		✔		NONE
New Jersey		✔		6 mos.
New Mexico	✔	✔		NONE
New York		✔		NONE

Chart 7 continued

Requirements for protecting your house from a nursing home

	An intent to return to the house	A doctor's certificate that you are expected to return	Even if you do not return to the house	Time limit on protection?
North Carolina		✔		6 mos.
North Dakota		✔		6 mos.
Ohio	✔			6 mos.
Oklahoma		✔		12 mos.
Oregon		✔		6 mos.
Pennsylvania	✔			NONE
Rhode Island	✔			NONE
South Carolina	✔			NONE
South Dakota	✔			NONE
Tennessee	✔			NONE
Texas	✔			NONE
Utah	✔			NONE
Vermont	✔			NONE
Virginia		✔		6 mos.
Washington	✔			NONE
West Virginia	✔			NONE
Wisconsin		✔		6 mos.
Wyoming	✔			NONE

1 Individuals who meet Florida residency requirements solely because they are institutionalized in a Medicaid facility but who own a home in another state may have that home excluded as an asset if either a spouse or a dependent relative resides in the home. It may also be excluded if the individual intends to return to that home and Florida has an interstate agreement with the state in which the home is located.

2 Massachusetts has just passed a law authorizing the Department of Public Welfare to place a lien on an individual's house upon entry into a nursing home. This currently does not apply to couples.

Please be aware that ALL states are increasingly targeting houses as a source of revenue and therefore this chart is subject to change constantly.

Chart 7   249

Chart 8

Assets considered non-countable when determining Medicaid eligibility

STATE	HOUSEHOLD GOODS	AUTOS [1]	RINGS	LIFE INSUR. [2]	BURIAL COSTS [3]
Alabama	Up to $4,000	2 regardless of value	Wedding rings only	Up to $2,500	Up to $2,500 if in burial account
Alaska	Up to $2,000	1 exempt, 2nd car can't exceed $4,500	1 wedding, 1 engagement	Up to $1,500	Up to $1,500 if in burial account
Arizona	Indiv. $2,000; Stay-at-home spouse no limit	1 exempt, 2nd car can't exceed $4,500	Up to $500; If more, amount deducted from $2,000 cash limit	Up to $1,500	Plot, no limit. Up to $1,500 if in burial account
Arkansas	Up to $2,000	1, can't exceed $4,500	Included in household goods' limit	Up to $1,500	Up to $1,500 if in burial account
California	No limit	1, no limit	No limit if not for investment	Up to $1,500	Up to $1,500 in both burial account and irrevocable trust
Colorado	No limit	No limit if used for medical purposes	No limit if not for investment	Up to $1,500	No limit if in an irrevocable trust
Connecticut	Up to $2,000	1, can't exceed $4,500	1 wedding, 1 engagement	Up to $1,500	Up to $1,000 if in burial account
Delaware	No limit	1 no limit	No limit if not for investment	Up to $1,500	Up to $1,500 if in burial account
DC	Up to $2,000	1, can't exceed $4,500	Up to $2,000	Up to $1,500	Plots and irrevocable contracts up to various limits
Florida	Up to $2,000	1, no limit	1 wedding, 1 engagement	Up to $2,500	Up to $2,500 for each spouse; Plots no limit

STATE	HOUSEHOLD GOODS	AUTOS [1]	RINGS	LIFE INSUR. [2]	BURIAL COSTS [3]
Georgia	Up to $2,000	1 excluded if used for medical purposes or employment	1 wedding, 1 engagement	Up to $1,500	Up to $5,000 if in burial account
Hawaii	No limit	1, up to $4,500	1 wedding, 1 engagement	Counts CSV against cash limit (see Chart 6)	Up to $1,500 if in irrevocable contract
Idaho	Up to 2000	1 exempt if used for medical purposes; 1 additional can't exceed $4,500	1 wedding, 1 engagement	Up to $1,500	Up to $1,500 if in burial account
Illinois	No limit	1, no limit	No limit if not for investment	Up to $1,500	Various
Indiana	No limit	1, no limit if for essential use	No limit if not for investment	Up to $1,400	No limit if in an irrevocable trust
Iowa	No limit	1, no limit	No limit if not for investment	Up to $1,500	Up to 1,500 if in burial account
Kansas	No limit	1, no limit	No limit if not for investment	Up to $1,500	Irrevocable burial contract no limit; Burial space/funds up to $1,500
Kentucky	No limit	1, no limit	No limit if not for investment	Up to $1,500	Up to $1,500 if in burial account. No limit if irrevocable life insurance policy
Louisiana	Up to $2,000	1, no limit if for essential use	1 wedding, 1 engagement	Up to $1,500	Plot, no limit; up to $1,500 if in burial account
Maine	No limit	1, no limit if for essential use	No limit if not for investment	Up to $1,500	No limit if reasonable
Maryland	No limit	1, no limit if for essential use	No limit if not for investment	Up to $1,500	No limit if reasonable

Assets considered non-countable when determining Medicaid eligibility *continued*

STATE	HOUSEHOLD GOODS	AUTOS [1]	RINGS	LIFE INSUR. [2]	BURIAL COSTS [3]
Massachusetts	No limit	1, no limit if for essential use	No limit if not for investment	Up to $1,500	Burial account up to $2,500; Pre-paid funeral no limit
Michigan	No limit	1, no limit	No limit if not for investment	Up to $1,000 in CSV. No limit if over 70	Up to $2,000 if in burial account
Minnesota	No limit	1, up to $4,500	No limit if not for investment	Up to $1,500	Up to $2,000 if in an irrevocable trust
Mississippi	No limit	1 up to $4,500	Up to $5,000	Up to $5,000	Up to $3,000 if in burial account
Missouri	No limit	1, no limit if for essential use	1 wedding, 1 engagement	Up to $1,500	No limit if in an irrevocable trust
Montana	Up to $2,000	1 excluded up to $4,500	1 wedding, 1 engagement	Up to $1,500	Up to $1,500 if in burial account
Nebraska	No limit	1, no limit	No limit if not for investment	Up to $1,500	Up to $3,000 if in burial account
Nevada	No limit	1, no limit if for essential use; If not up to $4,500	1 wedding, 1 engagement	Up to $1,500	Up to $1,500 if in burial account
New Hampshire	No limit	1, no limit if for essential use	1 wedding, 1 engagement	Up to $1,500	No limit if in an irrevocable contract
New Jersey	No limit	1, no limit if married; Up to $4,500 if single	1 wedding, 1 engagement	Up to $1,500	Up to $1,500 if in burial account
New Mexico	Up to $2,000	1, no limit if meets certain criteria	No limit if not for investment	Up to $1,500	Up to 1,500 if in burial account. Pre-paid funeral no limit
New York	No limit	1 no limit; 2nd, if spouse shows need	No limit if not for investment	Up to $1,500	Up to $1,500 if in burial account
North Carolina	No limit	1, up to $4,500	1 wedding, 1 engagement	All policies considered available	Up to $3,000 if in an irrevocable contract

STATE	HOUSEHOLD GOODS	AUTOS [1]	RINGS	LIFE INSUR. [2]	BURIAL COSTS [3]
North Dakota	No limit	1, no limit	No limit if not for investment	Up to $1,500	Up to $1,500 if in burial account
Ohio	No limit	1, no limit	No limit if not for investment	Up to $1,500	No limit if in irrevocable trust
Oklahoma	No limit	1, no limit if for essential use.	No limit if not for investment	Up to $1,500	Up to $6,000 if in irrevocable contract
Oregon	No limit	1 no limit for medical care; Otherwise up to $4,500	No limit if not for investment	Up to $1,500	Up to $1,500 for pre-paid funeral; Unlimited for burial merchandise
Pennsylvania	No limit	1, no limit if owned prior to application	No limit if not for investment	Up to $1,500	Up to $1,500 if in burial account; pre-paid no limit
Rhode Island	No limit	1, no limit if used for essential use; If not up to $4,500	No limit if not for investment	Up to $1,500	Plots no limit; Burial fund: up to $1,500
South Carolina	No limit	1, no limit	No limit if not for investment	Up to $1,500	No limit if in an irrevocable trust
South Dakota	No limit	1, up to $4,500 if essential for medical or employment	Up to $2,000	Up to $1,500	Pre-paid funeral up to $1,500
Tennessee	Up to $2,000	1, no limit if for essential use	No limit if not for investment	Up to $1,500	No limit if in an irrevocable trust
Texas	Up to $2,000	1 car, no limit for essential use; Otherwise up to $4,500	1 wedding, 1 engagement	Up to $1,500	Plots no limit; Up to $1,500 if in burial account
Utah	Up to $2,000	1, no limit if for essential use	Up to $500	Up to $1,500	Up to $1,500; if in burial account. Pre-paid no limit
Vermont	No limit	1, no limit if for essential use	No limit if not for investment	Up to $1,500; $3,000 for couple	Up to $1,500 if in burial account
Virginia	No limit	1 no limit	No limit if not for investment	Up to $1,500	Up to $2,500 if in burial fund

Assets considered non-countable when determining Medicaid eligibility *continued*

STATE	HOUSEHOLD GOODS	AUTOS [1]	RINGS	LIFE INSUR. [2]	BURIAL COSTS [3]
Washington	No limit	1, no limit if used for essential use; If not up to $4,500	No limit if not for investment	Up to $1,500	Up to $1,500 if in burial account. Plots no limit
West Virginia	No limit	1, no limit if used for essential use; otherwise $4,500	No limit if not for investment	Up to $1,500	Up to $1,500 if in burial account
Wisconsin	No limit	1, no limit if used for essential use; otherwise $4,500	No limit if not for investment	Up to $1,500	Up to 1,500 if in an irrevocable contract
Wyoming	Up to $2,000	1 car no limit	1 wedding	Up to $1,500	Up to $1,500 burial account. Plots no limit

1 Essential use generally means that the car must be used to go to a hospital, nursing home or for doctors' appointments. The states, however, are usually flexible in determining essential use.

2 Most states allow an individual or family to keep term policies regardless of their face value. A term policy has no cash surrender value and terminates on a person's failure to pay the premium. When reference is made to insurance policies having face values up to a certain amount in the chart, this means policies that have a cash surrender value. Some states count the cash surrender value toward the cash limit a person can keep (Chart 6). Some states deduct cash surrender value from the value of a burial account. Be sure to check with your local jurisdiction.

3 As you can see, each state has complex and confusing limits. In general, a burial account is a savings account with the following title: X in trust for Y. X could be a child or other individual and Y would be the person in a nursing home. These accounts are typically used to supplement irrevocable burial contracts (also referred to as pre-paid funerals). Massachusetts is a good example. It allows an individual to buy a pre-paid funeral in any amount and to supplement it with a burial account up to $2,500.

Many states allow an individual or couple to keep certain types of income-producing properties. Call your local Department of Public Welfare to find out how much equity these properties can have and whether or not they have to generate income in order to remain non-countable (exempt).

Chart 9

State Medicaid Offices

ALABAMA
Alabama Medicaid Agency
2500 Fairlane Drive
Montgomery, AL 36130
(205) 277-2710

ALASKA
Division of Medical Assistance
Dept of Health & Social Services
P.O. Box H
Juneau, AK 99811
(907) 465-3355

ARIZONA
Arizona Health Care Cost Containment
System (AHCCS)
801 East Jefferson
Pheonix, AZ 85034
(602) 244-3655

ARKANSAS
Arkansas Dept of Human Resources,
Medicaid
P.O. Box 1437
Little Rock, AR 72203
(501) 682-8502

CALIFORNIA
Medical Care Services
Dept of Health Services
714 P. Street, Room 1253
Sacramento, CA 95814
(916) 332-5824

COLORADO
Colorado Dept of Social Services
Health & Medical Services
1575 Sherman Street, 10th Floor
Denver, CO 80203
(303) 866-5901

CONNECTICUT
Dept of Income Maintenance
110 Bartholomew Avenue
Hartford, CT 06106
(203) 566-2008

DELAWARE
Division of Social Services
Dept of Health & Social Services,
Medicaid
1901 N. Dupont Highway, Briggs
Building
P.O. Box 906
New Castle, DE 19720
(302) 421-6140

FLORIDA
Medicaid Provider/Consumer Relations
1317 Winewood Boulevard
Building 6, Room 260
Tallahassee, FL 32399
(904) 488-8291

GEORGIA
Georgia Dept of Medical Assistance
2 Martin Luther King, Jr Drive
1220-C West Tower
Atlanta, GA 30334
(404) 656-4479

HAWAII
Health Care Administration
Dept of Human Services
P.O. Box 339
Honolulu, HI 96809
(808) 586-5392

IDAHO
Bureau of Welfare Medical Programs
Dept of Health & Welfare
450 W. State Street
Boise, ID 83720
(208) 334-5747

ILLINOIS
Division of Medical Programs
Illinois Dept of Public Aid
201 S. Grand Avenue East
Springfield, IL 62743
(217) 782-2570

INDIANA
Indiana State Dept of Public Welfare
100 N. Senate Avenue
State Office Building, Rm 701
Indianapolis, IN 46204
(317) 232-6865

IOWA
Division of Medical Services
Dept of Human Services
Hoover State Office Building
Des Moines, IA 50319
(515) 281-8621

KANSAS
Dept of Social & Rehabilitative
Services
Division of Medical Services
1915 Harrison Street
Docking State Office Building, Room
628-S
Topeka, KS 66612
(913) 296-3981

KENTUCKY
Dept of Medicaid Services
275 E. Main Street, 3rd Floor
Frankfort, KY 40621
(502) 564-4321

LOUISIANA
Bureau of Health Services Financing
P.O. Box 91031
Baton Rouge, LA 70821
(504) 342-3956

Chart 9   255

State Medicaid Offices

MAINE
Dept of Human Services
Bureau of Income Maintenance
State House Station #11
Whitten Road
Augusta, ME 04333
(207) 289-5088

MARYLAND
Medical Care Policy Administration
201 W. Preston Street
Baltimore, MD 21201
(301) 225-1432

MASSACHUSETTS
Dept of Public Welfare
180 Tremont Street, 13th Floor
Boston, MA 02111
(617) 574-0205

MICHIGAN
Medical Services Administration
Dept of Social Services
P.O. Box 30037
Lansing, MI 48909
(517) 335-5000

MINNESOTA
Dept of Human Services
Health Care Programs Division
444 Lafayette Road
St. Paul, MN 55155
(612) 296-8517

MISSISSIPPI
Division of Medicaid
801 Robert E. Lee Building
239 N. Lamar Street
Jackson, MS 39201
(601) 359-6050

MISSOURI
Division of Medical Services
Dept of Social Services
P.O. Box 6500
Jefferson City, MO 65102
(314) 751-3425

MONTANA
Medicaid Services Division
Dept of Social & Rehabilitation
Services
111 Sanders Street
P.O. Box 4210
Helena, MT 59604
(406) 444-4540

NEBRASKA
Nebraska Dept of Social Services
301 Centennial Mall South
P.O. Box 95026
Lincoln, NE 68509
(402) 471-3121

NEVADA
Division of Welfare
Dept of Human Resources
2527 N. Carson Street
Carson City, NV 89710
(702) 687-4378

NEW HAMPSHIRE
Division of Human Services
Office of Medical Services
6 Hazen Drive
Concord, NH 03301
(603) 271-4344

NEW JERSEY
Division of Medical Assistance &
Health Services
Dept of Human Services
CN-712
7 Quakerbridge Plaza
Trenton, NJ 08625
(609) 588-2600

NEW MEXICO
Medical Assistance Division
Dept of Human Services
P.O. Box 2348
Santa Fe, NM 87504
(505) 827-4315

NEW YORK
Division of Medical Assistance
New York State Dept of Social Services
40 N. Pearl Street
Albany, NY 12243
(518) 474-9132

NORTH CAROLINA
Division of Medical Assistance
Dept of Human Resources
1985 Umstead Drive
P.O. Box 29529
Raleigh, NC 27626
(919) 733-2060

NORTH DAKOTA
North Dakota Dept of Human Services
Medical Services
600 East Boulevard
Bismark, ND 58505
(701) 224-2321

OHIO
Dept of Human Services
Medicaid Administration
30 E. Broad Street, 31st Floor
Columbus, OH 43266
(614) 644-0140

OKLAHOMA
Division of Medical Services
Dept of Human Services
P.O. Box 25352
Oklahoma City, OK 73125
(405) 557-2539

State Medicaid Offices

OREGON
Office of Medical Assistance
Dept of Human Resources
203 Public Service Building
Salem, OR 97310
(503) 378-2263

PENNSYLVANIA
Dept of Public Welfare
Health & Welfare Building
P.O. Box 2675
Harrisburg, PA 17120
(717) 787-3119

RHODE ISLAND
Dept of Human Services
600 New London Avenue
Cranston, RI 02920
(401) 464-3575

SOUTH CAROLINA
South Carolina Health & Human
Services Finance Commission
1801 Main Street
Columbia, SC 29201
(803) 253-6128

SOUTH DAKOTA
Medical Services
Dept of Social Services
700 Governor's Drive
Kneip Building
Pierre, SD 57501
(605) 773-3495

TENNESSEE
Bureau of Medicaid
729 Church Street
Nashville, TN 37247
(615) 741-0213

TEXAS
Dept of Human Services
Health Care Services
P.O. Box 149030
Austin, TX 78714
(512) 450-3050

UTAH
Division of Health Care Financing
Utah Dept of Health
P.O. Box 16580
Salt Lake City, UT 84116
(801) 538-6151

VERMONT
Dept of Social Welfare
Vermont Agency of Human Services
103 S. Main Street
Waterbury, VT 05676
(802) 24102880

VIRGINIA
Virginia Dept of Medical Assistance
Services
600 E. Broad Street, Suite 1300
Richmond, VA 23212
(804) 786-7933

WASHINGTON
Medicaid Recipient Assistance &
Information
617 8th Avenue SE
Olympia, WA 98504
(800) 562-3022

WEST VIRGINIA
Division of Medical Care
West Virginia Dept of Human Services
State Capital Complex
Building 6, Room 717B
Charleston, WV 25305
(304) 348-8990

WISCONSIN
Division of Health
Wisconsin Dept of Health & Social
Services
P.O. Box 309
Madison, WI 53701
(608) 266-2522

WYOMING
Medical Assistance Services
Dept of Health & Social Services
6101 Yellowstone
Cheyenne, WY 82002
(307) 777-7531

DISTRICT OF COLUMBIA
Office of Health Care Financing
DC Dept of Human Services
2100 Martin Luther King, Jr Avenue SE
Suite 302
Washington, DC 20020
(202) 727-0735

**NORTHERN MARIANA
ISLANDS**
Dept of Community & Cultural Affairs
Office of the Governor
Saipan, CM 96950
(670) 332-9722

PUERTO RICO
Dept of Social Services
P.O. Box 11398
Santurce, PR 00910
(809) 722-7400

VIRGIN ISLANDS
Dept of Human Services
Barbel Plaza South
St. Thomas, VI 00802
(809)774-0930

Chart 9   257

Chart 10

State Insurance Commission Addresses

ALABAMA
135 South Union Street #160
Montgomery, Alabama 36130- 3401
1-205-269-3550

ALASKA
P.O. Box D
Juneau, Alaska 99811
1-907-465-2515

AMERICAN SAMOA
Office of the Governor
Pago Pago, American Samoa
96796
1-684-633-4116

ARIZONA
3030 No. 3rd St., Suite 1100
Phoenix, Arizona 85012
1-602-255-5400

ARKANSAS
400 University Tower Bldg.
12th & University Street
Little Rock, Arkansas 72204
1-501-371-1325

CALIFORNIA
100 Van Ness Avenue
San Francisco, California 94102
1-415-557-9624

COLORADO
303 West Colfax Avenue
5th Floor
Denver, Colorado 80204
1-303-620-4300

CONNECTICUT
165 Capitol Avenue
State Office Building
Room 425
Hartford, Connecticut 06106
1-203-566-5275

DELAWARE
841 Silverlake Boulevard
Dover, Delaware 19901
1-302-736-4251

DISTRICT OF COLUMBIA
613 G. Street, NW
6th Floor
Washington, D.C. 20001
1-202-727-5422

FLORIDA
State Capitol
Plaza Level Eleven
Tallahassee, Florida 32399-0300
1-904-488-3440

GEORGIA
2 Martin L. King, Jr. Dr.
704 West Tower
Atlanta, Georgia 30334
1-404-656-2056

GUAM
P.O. Box 2796
Agana, Guam 96910
or 855 West Marine Drive
011-671-477-1040

HAWAII
P.O. Box 3614
Honolulu, Hawaii 96811
1-808-548-5450

IDAHO
500 South 10th Street
Boise, Idaho 83720
1-208-334-2250

ILLINOIS
320 West Washington St. 4th Flr.
Springfield, Illinois 62767
1-217-782-4515

INDIANA
311 West Washington Street
Suite 300
Indianapolis, Indiana 46204-2787
1-317-232-2386

IOWA
Lucas State Office Building
6th Floor
Des Moines, Iowa 50319
1-515-281-5705

State Insurance Commission Addresses (continued)

KANSAS
420 S.W. 9th Street
Topeka, Kansas 66612
1-913-296-7801

KENTUCKY
229 West Main Street
P.O. Box 517
Frankfort, Kentucky 40602
1-501-564-3630

LOUISIANA
P.O. Box 94214
Baton Rouge, Louisiana 70804- 9214
or 950 North 5th Street
Baton Rouge, Louisiana
70804- 9214
1-504-342-5328

MAINE
State Office Building
State House, Station 34
Augusta, Maine 04333
1-207-582-8707

MARYLAND
501 St. Paul Place
(Stanbalt Bldg.)
7th Floor-South
Baltimore, Maryland 21202
1-301-333-2520

MASSACHUSETTS
280 Friend Street
Boston, Massachusetts 02114
1-617-727-7189

MICHIGAN
P.O. Box 30220
Lansing, Michigan 48909
or 611 West Ottawa Street
2nd Floor,
North Lansing, Michigan 48933
1-517-373-9273

MINNESOTA
500 Metro Square Building
5th Floor
St. Paul, Minnesota 55101
1-612-296-6848

MISSISSIPPI
1804 Walter Sillers Bldg.
P.O. Box 79
Jackson, Mississippi 39205
1-601-359-3569

MISSOURI
301 West High Street 6 North
P.O. Box 690
Jefferson City, Missouri
65102-0690
1-314-751-2451

MONTANA
126 North Sanders
Mitchell Building
Room 270
P.O. Box 4009
Helena, Montana 59601
1-406-444-2040

NEBRASKA
Terminal Building
941 O Street, Suite 400
Lincoln, Nebraska 68508
1-402-471-2201

NEVADA
Nye Building
201 South Fall Street
Carson City, Nevada 89701
1-702-885-4270

NEW HAMPSHIRE
169 Manchester Street
Concord, New Hampshire 03301
1-603-271-2261

NEW JERSEY
20 West State Street CN325
Trenton, New Jersey 08625
1-609-292-5363

NEW MEXICO
Pera Bldg.
P.O. Drawer 1269
Santa Fe, New Mexico
87504-1269
1-505-827-4500

NEW YORK
160 West Broadway
New York, New York 10013
1-212-602-0429

NORTH CAROLINA
Capitol Bldg.
Fifth Floor
Bismarck, North Dakota 58505
1-701-224-2440

OHIO
2100 Stella Court
Columbus, Ohio 43266-0566
1-614-644-2658

Chart 10 259

State Insurance Commission Addresses (continued)

OKLAHOMA
P.O. Box 53408
Oklahoma City, Oklahoma
73152-3404
or 1901 North Walnut
Oklahoma City, Oklahoma 73105
1-405-521-2828

OREGON
21 Labor & Industries Bldg.
Salem, Oregon 97310
1-503-378-4271

PENNSYLVANIA
Strawberry Square
13th Floor
Harrisburg, Pennsylvania 17120
1-717-787-5173

PUERTO RICO
Fernandez Juncos Station
P.O. Box 8330
Santurce, PR 00910
1-809-722-8686

RHODE ISLAND
233 Richmond St., Suite 237
Providence, Rhode Island
02903-4237
1-401-277-2246

SOUTH CAROLINA
1612 Marion Street
Columbia, South Carolina 29201
or P.O. Box 100105
Columbia, South Carolina 29202-
3105
1-803-737-6117

SOUTH DAKOTA
Insurance Building
910 E. Sioux Avenue
Pierre, South Dakota 57501
1-605-773-3563

TENNESSEE
Volunteer Plaza
500 James Robertson Pkwy.
Nashville, Tennessee 37219
1-615-741-2241

TEXAS
1110 San Jacinto Blvd.
Austin, Texas 78701-1998
1-512-463-9979

UTAH
P.O. Box 45803
Salt Lake City, Utah 84145
or 160 E. Third Street
Heber M. Wells Bldg.
Salt Lake City, Utah 84145
1-801-530-6400

VERMONT
State Office Building
Montpelier, Vermont 05602
1-802-828-3301

VIRGINIA
700 Jefferson Building
P.O. Box 1157
Richmond, Virginia 23209
1-804-786-3741

VIRGIN ISLANDS
Kongens Gade #18
St. Thomas, V.I. 00802
1-809-774-2991

WASHINGTON
Insurance Building AQ21
Olympia, Washington 98504
1-206-753-7301

WEST VIRGINIA
2019 Washington Street, E
Charleston, West Virginia 25305
1-304-348-3394

WISCONSIN
P.O. Box 7873
123 West Washington Ave.
Madison, Wisconsin 53702
1-608-266-0102

WYOMING
Herschler Building
122 West 25th Street
Cheyenne, Wyoming 82002
1-307-777-7401

CHAPTER 17

RESOURCES

Living wills

- Over 40 states now have statutes that require a specific form for a living will. For a free copy of the official living will form for your state and guidelines for its use, send a *stamped self-addressed envelope* to

> The Society for the Right to Die
> Department NL, Suite 831
> 250 West 57th Street
> New York, NY 10107

- Doctors Linda and Ezekiel Emmanuel, husband and wife physicians affiliated with Massachusetts General Hospital, have designed a comprehensive document that helps clarify what measures you would allow in a variety of different illness scenarios. Called a "Medical Directive," it outlines your values and preferences and deals with naming a proxy and communicating with your doctor. Write to:

> *Medical Directive*
> Harvard Health Letter
> PO Box 380
> Boston , MA 02117
> Send $5.00 for minimum order of two copies.

Finding a lawyer

- A free booklet, *Questions and Answers When Looking for an Elder Law Attorney*, can be obtained by sending a stamped, self-addressed envelope to:

  National Academy of Elder Law Attorneys
  655 N. Alvernon Way, Suite 108
  Tucson, AZ 85711

- Referrals: For a name or names of an elder law attorney in your state, see the form on page 274.

Books for caregivers

- *How to Care for Your Aging Parents*
  A Handbook for Adult Children
  Nora Jean Levin
  The kind of short guide that should be in every family's bookcase. 103 pages, $5.95.

  Storm King Press
  Box 3566
  Washington, DC 20007

- *You and Your Aging Parent*
  A Family Guide to Emotional, Physical & Financial Problems
  Barbara Silverstone and Helen Kandel Hyman
  A helpful guide through the maze of emotional and practical problems of caregiving. 351 pages, $14.95.
  Pantheon Books
  Available in bookstores.

- *How to Survive Your Aging Parent*
  ...so you and *they can enjoy life.*
  Bernard H. Shulman, M.D. and Raeann Berman
  A compassionate look at the frustrations, anxieties and rewards of caregiving. 192 pages,$10.95.
  Surrey Books
  101 East Erie Street
  Chicago, IL 60611

- *Talking with Your Aging Parents*
  Mark A. Edinberg
  How to communicate with your parents about troublesome subjects like nursing homes, legal and financial matters, and death. 220 pages, $9.95.

  Shambhala Publications
  300 Massachusetts Avenue
  Boston, MA 02115

Help for caregivers

Children of Aging Parents (CAPS)
A national clearinghouse for care givers of the elderly and for professionals in the field of aging. Support groups, a hotline, a newsletter and more. Membership: Individual – $15.
Professional or organizations – $25.

2761 Trenton Road
Levittown, PA 19056
215 945-6900

Especially for seniors

• *American Guidance for Seniors*
Ken Skala
You can take advantage of the many state, federal and private programs for the elderly but only if you know about them. This is an indispensable handbook of benefits, entitlements, and assistance for Americans over age sixty. An excellent resource. 531 pages, $15.95 plus $4.00 postage and handling.

American Guidance, Inc.
6231 Leesburg Pike, Suite 305
Falls Church, VA 22044

- *How to Keep Control of Your Life After 50*
  A guide for your legal, medical, and financial well-being
  Offers the knowledge and the tools necessary for
  elderly people to get what they want – in their
  medical treatment, their finances, and in making
  important decisions. 428 pages, $17.95.

  Macmillan Publishing Company
  100 Front Street
  Box 500 Riverside, NJ 08075-7500

- *ElderLaw News* (four-page quarterly newsletter)
  A readable four-page newsletter presenting elder
  law developments and estate planning techniques
  for the general public.

  ElderLaw News
  101 Arch Street
  Boston, MA 02110
  $15 for a one-year subscription

For professionals

- *The Medicaid Planning Handbook*
  Alexander A. Bove, Jr., Esq.
  Two versions, one for professionals, the other for
  lay people. *Covers Massachusetts only.* $23 plus $3.50
  for postage and handling.

  Ormand Sacker Press
  P.O. Box 4526, Boston, MA 02101

- *Aging and the Law*
Peter Strauss, Robert Wolf and Dana Shilling
An excellent comprehensive resource for professionals — lawyers, accountants, insurance consultants, physicians, social workers, gerontologists. 912 pages, $100.

Commerce Clearing House, Inc.
4025 West Peterson Avenue
Chicago, IL 60646
1 800 248-3248

- *The ElderLaw Report*
An in-depth, up-to-date monthly report on legal developments and planning techniques that the elder law professional needs to know.

The ElderLaw Report
Little Brown and Company
Law Division
34 Beacon Street
Boston, MA 02108
8 to 12 pages, $89 for one year.

- *1991 Medicaid Source Book: Background Data and Analysis*
  The report prepared by the Congressional Research Service
  Available in fall 1991 from:

  The Government Printing Office
  Washington, DC 20402
  202 783-3238

- *Long-Term Care Insurance*
  A professional's guide to selecting policies
  Susan E. Polniaszek and James P. Firman
  Two experts cut through the fog and confusion. 91 pages, $35.00 plus $1.50 postage and handling.

  United Seniors Health Cooperative
  1331 H Street, NW #500
  Washington, DC 20005
  202 393-6222

Agencies

- Your Office of Elder Affairs (in your phone book under government)
- Your state Division of Insurance (see page 258)
- Your local Department of Public Welfare (the name varies state by state. It may also be called the Department of Social Services, the Department of Economic Security, or any of a handful of other similar names (see page 255)

Insurance

- *Long-Term Care: A Dollar and Sense Guide*
  A short but thorough look at the pros and cons of long-term care insurance. Helps answer the question, Is nursing home insurance a good idea for me? 72 pages, $8.50 plus $1.50 for postage and handling.

  United Seniors Health Cooperative
  1331 H Street, Suite 500, Washington, D.C. 20005
  202 393-6222

- *A Shopper's Guide to Long-Term Care Insurance*
  A booklet of basic non-critical information including a helpful policy comparison checklist. First copy free.

  National Association of Insurance Commissioners
  120 West 12th Street
  Kansas City, MO 64105

- Reprint: The June 1991 *Consumer Reports* article entitled: "The Traps in Long-Term Care Insurance". Send $3.00 to:

  Consumer Reports/Reprints
  101 Truman Avenue
  Yonkers, NY
  10703-1057

- *A.M. Best's Insurance Report*

  Perhaps the most widely used reference of this sort. It evaluates insurance companies' relative financial strength using six ratings from Superior (A+), Excellent (A or A-), Very Good (B+), Good (B or B-), Fairly Good (C), or Fair (C or C-). You can look up any company by going to your local library. Your librarian can direct you to two other rating sources, Standard and Poor's and Moody's, as well.

Books on the issues

- *Risking Old Age In America*

  Richard J. Margolis

  A Families USA Foundation Book

  A beautiful, warm book that puts human faces on the facts and statistics of aging. If the issues facing the elderly don't particularly interest you, reading this book will raise your consciousness and move you to the heart. Part sociological treatise, part touching narrative, this work is an example of how a gifted writer can make any subject compelling. 202 pages. $14.95 plus $3.00 for postage and handling.

  Westview Press
  5500 Central Avenue
  Boulder, Colorado 80301
  1 800 456-1995

Books on the issues
continued

• *Caring for the Disabled Elderly*
Who will pay?
Alice M. Rivlin and Joshua M. Wiener
An examination of possible solutions to the
problem of financing long-term care. 318 pages.

Brookings Institution
1775 Massachusetts Avenue, NW
Washington, DC 20036

• Critical Issues
A National Health System for America
edited by Stuart M. Butler and Edmund F.
Haislmaier
A strategy to make adequate, affordable health
care available to every American. 127 pages, $8.00.

The Heritage Foundation
Publications Department
214 Massachusetts Avenue, NE
Washington, DC 20002
202 546-4400

For corporations

The Dependent Care Connection
Employee *counseling services*
A national child care and elder care information/referral/counseling service providing assistance to workers through employer participation.

Dependent Care Connection
PO Box 2783
Westport, CT 06880
203 226-2680

Support services

Alzheimer's Disease & Related Disorders Association

70 East Lake Street, Suite 600
Chicago, IL 60601
1 800 621-0379
In Illinois, 1 800 527-6037

A source for referrals to local chapters and support groups.

Support services
continued

Arthritis Foundation
1314 Spring Street, NW
Atlanta, GA 30309
1 800 283-7800

A source for referrals to local chapters, support groups, doctors and clinics.

National Parkinson Foundation
1501 NW 9th Avenue
Miami, FL 33136
305 547-6666
1 800 327-4545

Health Information Center
PO Box 1133
Washington, DC 20013
1 800 336-4797

A source for information and help for a wide variety of health problems. A good starting place for referrals.

Health hotlines

There are at least 300 health-related hotlines that provide assistance free of charge. People coping with Alzheimer's, arthritis, cancer, heart disease, osteoporosis or many other health problems can find help in a directory of health hotlines. To receive a copy, write to:

Health Hotlines
Public Information Office
National Library of Medicine
Bethesda, MD 20894

You may cut out this form or photocopy it (both sides) and then fill it out.

Request for Referral

I would like to find an attorney who is familiar with the field of elder law. Please send one or more names and addresses of attorneys in my area whom I can call for help.

Name
- -

Number and Street
- -

City/town
- -

State   Zip   Ph
- -

A large metropolitan area close to me is: - - - - - - - - - - - - - - - - -

I have questions regarding: (circle one or more)

1) Estate planning, including wills and trusts
2) Guardianship/conservatorship
3) Medicaid planning

I have enclosed $12.00 to cover research, postage and handling.

Please read the following carefully:

This service is offered to provide additional resources to readers of this book in the form of elder law attorneys. Financial Planning Institute, Inc., Harley Gordon, and Jane Daniel do not receive any referral fee or other compensation of any nature from the attorneys whose names are given out. The authors have taken reasonable steps to assure that the lawyers whose names are provided through this service are experienced in the area of elder law. No warranty, express or implied, is made as to their competency.

We will try to give you names close to your address, however this may not always be possible.

Please read and sign

I agree to take reasonable steps to verify the competency of any attorney I engage.

By signing this letter, I release Financial Planning Institute, Inc., and the authors of this book from any liability that might arise from this referral.

Signed: _____ Date: _____

(Referrals cannot be processed without your signature.)

Mail to: Financial Planning Institute
       PO Box 135
       Boston, MA 02258

Please allow up to three weeks for a response.

INDEX

NOTES: